MAKING
SENSE
OF
MONEY

5/5/23

To John,
Thanks so much for
your friendship over the
many years! Hope you
enjoy the book!!
Leave a legacy,
Jim

MAKING
SENSE
OF
MONEY

HOW TO OUTSMART INFLATION,
BUILD FINANCIAL SECURITY,
AND LEAVE A LEGACY

JAMES C. WHITEHURST III

CLEARSIGHT
BOOKS

Raleigh, North Carolina

ISBN hardback: 978-1-945209-30-7

ISBN paperback: 978-1-945209-31-4

ISBN ebook: 978-1-945209-32-1

Library of Congress Control Number: 2022916893

Published by Clear Sight Books, Raleigh, North Carolina

Book and Cover Design by Patricia Saxton

To my wife and family, including my Coastal family,
who inspire me every day.

To my children, who I hope will leave their own legacy
through investing and helping others.

CONTENTS

INTRODUCTION

AMERICANS ARE NOT good with money.

More than half of Americans have less than three months' worth of expenses in an emergency fund; one quarter indicate having no emergency fund at all.[1]

Do those numbers surprise you?

In a 2021 survey, only 18 percent of people near retirement age said they were on track with their savings, and 53 percent expected to keep working in order to cover their daily expenses.[2]

Are you concerned by those stats?

Most shocking of all: nearly two-thirds of Americans live paycheck to paycheck regardless of their income.[3]

Does that statement hit a little too close to home?

The truth is, if you don't steward your money, build savings, and invest to outpace the rate of inflation, you are effectively *losing* money—and with it, financial security for yourself and your family.

WHO THIS BOOK IS FOR

In *Making Sense of Money*, my goal is to help you look at your finances in a fresh light and give you the confidence to take steps towards building financial security and wealth. Maybe you are:

- Just beginning your professional life and don't have much experience with managing money.
- Tired of living paycheck to paycheck.
- Worried you don't have enough saved for retirement.
- Happy with your savings account but nervous about investing.
- Interested in leaving a legacy to your church or faith organization, or to a nonprofit or a cause you care about, but don't know if you will have enough money to do so.

If you are ready to take control of your money and improve your financial position, this book is for you.

WHAT YOU WILL LEARN

Making Sense of Money is intended to help you think broadly about how you manage your money and the opportunities that exist for you. It offers practical advice without overwhelming you with too much detail.

In Part One, we'll assess where you are currently. We'll explore what it means to be "good with money," influences on our relationship with money, and the five money personalities.

In Part Two, we'll focus on building financial discipline. We'll look at key concepts for financial literacy; money habits, good and bad; and the Wealth Pyramid, your blueprint for building wealth.

Finally in Part Three, we'll look at investing in the stock market, which is your best bet for beating inflation and building wealth. We'll cover types of investments and their relative risk, and the basics of stock market investing.

By the end of the book, you will have a solid place to begin making the changes needed to build wealth and security for yourself and your family and to leave a legacy for them and others. In addition, you'll have a list of useful resources to consult as you continue your financial journey.

WHY LISTEN TO ME

I believe wealth should be about security, not happiness. Money alone cannot make you truly happy, and there are many "carpe diem" folks who don't worry about this stuff at all. But for anyone who wants greater financial security, and with it greater opportunity to find happiness, I hope that this book can be a springboard for action.

As a second-generation family business owner, I owe my parents and grandparents a debt of gratitude. I grew up in a family of investors. Even during the Great Depression of the 1930s my grandparents continued to invest in the stock market. I can't imagine how much faith that must have taken after the crash of 1929. They were raising my dad and his two younger siblings on a small farm in North Carolina; since they grew their own food, they never went hungry, but still—those must have been lean times. Even so, in 1953 my grandparents were able to loan my father $10,000 to start an agricultural supply business.

The elder generations continued teaching the younger to be smart investors. From the time I was about ten, I can remember our family owning Eli Lilly and Company stock and playing "the stock market game" in which each player would try to accumulate the most shares (not unlike Monopoly). Learning about the market at such a young age brought a level of comfort with investing that served me well when I was old enough to invest for myself.

In college I studied economics and business, and then, after working in banking for a year, I returned to help manage the family business. The business grew over the years from that bare minimum investment to eight figures and then to nine figures. I continue to run the business today—and it's still growing.

Without my grandparents' diligence with saving and investing wisely, I never would have had the opportunity to continue my father's legacy; my gratitude is one reason for writing this book.

The other, perhaps more relevant, reason for writing this book is my deep-seated desire to help people be better stewards of their hard-earned money. The statistics at the beginning of this introduction don't lie: too many Americans possess poor knowledge of all things financial and are missing out on the lifelong benefits of financial literacy. I think deeply about finance—both personal and business—on a regular basis, and I can't help but believe I might have something to offer. The knowledge and experience I started accumulating as a child have compounded for me over the years to where I am today—in a position to make my dreams a reality.

I don't represent any financial company, and I haven't been paid a dime by any of the companies or people mentioned in this book. Nor do I expect to make a profit from this endeavor. I'm simply sharing my financial experience, research, and approach, as well as some excellent resources, without the bias you might find from someone trying to sell you something. I'm writing purely for your benefit.

If you're ready to become a better steward of your money so you can increase your family's financial security, expand your opportunities, and maybe even leave a legacy . . . welcome.

PART ONE

ARE YOU GOOD WITH MONEY?

IN PART ONE, WE'LL LOOK at what it means to be "good with money" and some of the underlying reasons we may not be so good with money. We'll also describe the five core money personalities. When you recognize yourself, you can better see patterns of behavior that you might like to reinforce—or change.

CHAPTER 1

BEING GOOD WITH MONEY

"IF YOU HAVE NOT ACQUIRED MORE THAN A BARE
EXISTENCE IN THE YEARS SINCE WE WERE YOUTHS,
IT IS BECAUSE YOU EITHER HAVE FAILED TO LEARN
THE LAWS THAT GOVERN THE BUILDING OF WEALTH,
OR ELSE YOU DO NOT OBSERVE THEM."
—GEORGE S. CLASON,
THE RICHEST MAN IN BABYLON (1926)

HUNTINGTON (HUNT) HARTFORD was born in 1911 into one of the wealthiest families in the United States. His grandfather George was one of the co-founders of The Great Atlantic & Pacific Tea Company (A&P) and was instrumental in its phenomenal growth. When Hunt was born, there were 400 A&P stores; by 1930, there were approximately 16,000 grocery store locations and A&P had become the first $1 billion retailer. In 1917, Hunt's grandfather died, leaving him a trust fund that generated an annual income of about $1.5 million (the equivalent of about $34 million today). Hunt's two uncles ran and grew the business, but Hunt himself lasted only about six months at A&P. Nonetheless, by the early 1960s, he was one of America's richest men. As one of the big American playboys, he befriended John Jacob Astor IV and Charlie Chaplin, as well as business rivals Howard Hughes and Aristotle Onassis. He socialized with Doris Duke, Lana Turner, and Marilyn Monroe, and owned homes in Los Angeles, Palm Beach, London, and Manhattan. He spent his fortune on fine art, the theater, and purchasing and attempting to develop Paradise Island, Bahamas. By about 1980, his $500 million inheritance was all but gone.

Ronald Read was born in 1921 on a small farm in the tiny town of Dummerston, Vermont. He walked or hitchhiked four miles to school and was the first high school graduate in his family. He served in the US Army in WWII, and after the war, he settled in Brattleboro, Vermont. He worked as a gas station attendant for twenty-five years and then as a janitor at the local J. C. Penney for another seventeen years. Ron lived an extremely frugal lifestyle, even using a safety pin on his tattered winter coat to avoid buying a new one. From his appearance and lack of material belongings, the locals assumed he was poor. However, Ron had a hobby that few people knew about: investing. He enjoyed reading the *Wall Street Journal* and *Barron's* every day during his visits to the local library and owned nearly one hundred stocks at the time of his death in 2014. When his executor opened his safe deposit box, she found a five-inch-thick stack of stock certificates he had tucked away over the years. He had an estate worth $8 million, built mostly from investing in the stock market. He left part of it to his stepchildren, but the majority of it went to the local library and hospital.

Boris Becker, the winner of six Grand Slam tennis championships, at one time had an estimated net worth of $100 to $150 million accumulated from his success as an athlete. His post-tennis career, however, has been disastrous. An extravagant lifestyle and huge divorce settlements helped lead the way to Becker's eventual downfall. He was convicted of tax evasion and forced into bankruptcy by a London court, and in 2022, he was sentenced to prison for bankruptcy-related offenses. Boris and his combustible lifestyle certainly lived up to his nickname on the court: "Boom Boom."

Barbara Corcoran grew up in New Jersey in a family of ten children with an alcoholic father. She did poorly in school, as she suffered from dyslexia and likely other learning disorders. Nicknamed "the dumb kid," she was a D student all the way through high school. However, she overcame her learning issues with perseverance and imagination and by outworking everyone else. She started her own company with a $1,000 loan from a boyfriend, and later sold the business for $66 million. She's now best known as one of the "sharks" on the TV show *Shark Tank*.

In 1982, John McConnell was fired by the software company he worked for and decided to start his own medical software company with $25,000, two partners, and a house pledged to secure a line of credit. It was a tenuous start. McConnell and his partners got a lead for a Michigan consulting company that was interested in their software, so they set out on the thirteen-hour drive from North Carolina to Michigan to make their pitch. The meeting went well and the consulting company was impressed. The prospective client insisted on driving them back to the airport, even after they said, "Nah, that's not necessary." Suffice it to say, they took a cab from the airport back to the office to retrieve their car for the long drive back to

Raleigh. Medic Computer Systems grew into the largest company in the country for physician office software and was sold in 1997 for $923 million.

Whether you make money as an entrepreneur like Barbara Corcoran, inherit wealth like Hunt Hartford, make money quickly like Boris Becker, or never spend and simply accumulate money like Ronald Read, the route to wealth (or lack thereof) lies with you. Luckily, between these extreme examples lies a wide range of "normal."

Personal finance is indeed quite personal, and proprietary to each one of us. How we manage our household budget, whether we choose to go into debt or pay with cash only, and how we manage our investments are all individual, personal decisions. So we can choose to be good with money, or not.

MAYBE WE'RE NOT SO GOOD WITH MONEY

What does it mean to be "good with money"? Does it mean having specialized knowledge or being a financial whiz, or is it having the fortitude to save rather than spend? Is easy credit the culprit for our poor habits, or should we assume more personal responsibility for controlling our spending?

In my opinion, being good with money means making decisions that lead to financial security for you and your family.

I have read so many personal finance books that it would be impossible to list them all. Without exception, the advice about how to get control of your finances consists of what I would consider common sense: live within your means, and spend less than you earn. That's good advice, but it seems few people act on it. The US is one of the richest countries on earth. Why is it that 40 percent of Americans have essentially zero net worth[4] and 56 percent could not come up with an immediate $1,000 to handle a repair?[5] How is it possible that nearly a third of people making over $100,000 per year are living paycheck to paycheck?[6] Even doctors, who many people assume are rich, are often not. Most doctors do have a high income, but often not until their mid to late thirties. By the time they've bought a nice house and car and paid for the kids' school (not to mention malpractice insurance), their annual income is largely spent. The result can be little net worth. In other words, they look the part of a millionaire even though they may not be one.

This dilemma has always intrigued me. Are some of us simply lucky? Or do we make our own luck by taking advantage of opportunity? Do most folks just not possess common sense? Or does personal finance require something more than common sense? What *is* common sense exactly?

Common sense is commonly defined along the lines of "sound judgment not based on specialized knowledge"[7] or "practical judgment derived from experience rather than just from study alone."[8] It serves us fine for navigating everyday life: We don't leave our house on a freezing day without our coat. We lock our doors at night. We buckle our seat belts (the car will beep obnoxiously if we don't). We taste our food before we add salt. (Right?) We don't attempt to drive through a flooded road when there are flash flood warnings. We spend less money than we earn. Huh? That's what the minimum payments on my credit card are for!

Clearly, common sense is not so common when it comes to managing our money. If managing our money were based on common sense, that is, sound judgment gained through experience, then we wouldn't buy stuff we couldn't afford. In Duncan J. Watts's excellent book *Everything Is Obvious: Once You Know the Answer*, he states, "For something we refer to so often . . . common sense is surprisingly hard to pin down." Financial common sense seems to be what we believe the other guy should know: "Spend less than you earn" and "Don't buy it if you can't pay for it." Yet these basic principles get crushed when emotional buying jumps in.

Watts further notes: "Common sense . . . is not so much a worldview as a grab bag of logically inconsistent, often contradictory beliefs, each of which seems right at the time but carries no guarantee of being right any other time." In other words, common sense leads us down a path of decision-making that sounds good and provides a nice story to fit our narrative and rationalize our behaviors.

I contend that relying on common sense alone leaves us far short of meeting our financial goals. When it comes to making sense of money, what should be obvious and intuitive to each of us is often challenging. If you've ever listened to finance guru Dave Ramsey's radio show, you know that when callers ask questions, the answer to us (the listeners) is fairly obvious (that is, it's common sense), but the caller is baffled. Dave normally requires the caller to answer their own question, just like Glenda the Good Witch does with Dorothy in *The Wizard of Oz*: the answer is simple, but she has to figure it out for herself. Given the chance to reflect, we can usually understand what common sense should have told us—and why we didn't use it.

WE NEED MORE THAN FINANCIAL
COMMON SENSE

So, if we can't count on common sense alone to lead us to sound money management decisions, what else is required? Intelligence? Is there some innate financial intelligence gene? Good question.

In *The* Next *Millionaire Next Door*, the sequel to the 1996 bestseller *The Millionaire Next Door* from Thomas J. Stanley, PhD, and William D. Danko, PhD, Stanley's daughter, Sarah Stanley Fallaw, PhD, reveals the intriguing finding that being a millionaire is not correlated with intelligence. *Income* is correlated with intelligence, but *wealth* is not. (I highly recommend this book and its wonderful research.) So if sound money decisions are not that "common" and building wealth is not tied to our IQ, then what gives? Dr. Fallaw makes the case that *frugality* is the key driver to success at building wealth.

Ronald Read sacrificed his entire life in the name of frugality. Perhaps Ron was entirely happy with his lifestyle (it seems he was), but I'm not sure most of us would be comfortable living at quite that level of thriftiness. Nevertheless, many of us could add a good dose of frugality to our lives and be none the worse for wear.

Approaching the 2008 Great Recession, the personal savings rate in the United States had declined to a historic low of around 4 percent.[9] The rate climbed during the COVID-19 pandemic due to stimulus payments as well as the normal tendency to save during uncertain times, but I am not optimistic that it will remain high. I suspect that post-pandemic we will gradually fall back to abysmally low 4 percent levels until the next crisis hits.

Rather than maintaining at least modest frugality and building our savings, we often let our emotions drive our decisions and spend, spend, spend. The "keeping up with the Joneses" effect shows up regularly. We attend a friend's dinner party and invariably leave with new items on our "gotta have it" list. Not only the house itself, but also the furniture, the landscaping, the artwork. Common sense and frugality get left behind at the party when one spouse envisions a new theater room and the other dreams of a condo at the beach.

But let's give ourselves the benefit of the doubt and say we've become more frugal. I would argue this is not enough—we can still make poor money decisions if we lack financial literacy.

Do you know what these terms mean: *Rule of 72, real rate of return, 15-year amortization*, and *compound interest*? If you're not familiar with them, don't worry—by the end of this book, you will be. They'll help you understand how money works and how wealth (and financial security) is built over time.

We often conveniently substitute common sense for the acquisition of knowledge. We decide something is "true" because our common sense told us so, therefore relieving us of the burden of further study to help analyze a key financial purchase. But the car or boat salesperson couldn't care less about our financial well-being and aims their sales pitch right at our "common sense."

Nothing about personal finance is very complicated. Yes, you must build a base of knowledge to succeed at it, but isn't that true of anything worthwhile? It's disheartening to know that we do such a poor job of financial education in our classrooms. As of 2021, only twenty-one states required high school students to take a personal finance course.[10] In North Carolina, we are starting to make headway with a required course in high school, and I think the Suze Ormans and Dave Ramseys of the world do an excellent job teaching people financial concepts, but we've got a long way to go.

To build wealth, common sense is not enough. To be "good with money," we need something more.

WE NEED FINANCIAL DISCIPLINE

Discipline is defined as "the practice of training people to obey rules or a code of behavior, using punishment to correct disobedience" or "a branch of knowledge, typically one studied in higher education."[11] My premise is that being "good with money" requires developing financial discipline, which has three components: gaining financial literacy, managing our money habits, and following a financial plan.

Gaining Financial Literacy. One definition of discipline relates to learned knowledge (and we already noted that financial matters are not taught very well in school). We must gain enough knowledge to make better-informed decisions. Financial literacy falls somewhere between practical knowledge and specialized knowledge such as that gained through years of training in fields like medicine and law. For example, as a business owner I must have some basic knowledge about the law to know what is legal or not legal. I don't call a lawyer every time we need to consider the law, because I have a certain amount of training to be comfortable in making a good decision.

It's the same when making a key purchasing decision. If I'm buying insurance, I don't need to know everything my agent knows about all the options and considerations. But if I don't know *anything* about insurance and I ask my neighbor or relative what to do because I trust him, how wise is that? What does he really know about insurance? And a product that may be a fit for him might not work for me. If I rely too much on my agent, then I may end up with more (or worse, less) coverage than I need. So having some specialized knowledge comes in handy for making a decision that's good for you and your family. But there are no shortcuts—as my mother always told me, you must "Read, read, read!" to increase your financial vocabulary and acumen.

We'll discuss financial literacy more in Chapter 4.

Managing Our Money Habits. It's possible to be financially literate and still make poor buying decisions. Why? Because we put our emotions in charge of our purchasing habits. We make impulse decisions when we get in too big a hurry and a good salesperson is involved. It has been estimated that the average American spends over $250 per month on impulse purchases.[12] The urge to buy now and save later is a strong one, what with the convenience of credit and credit cards. The YOLO (You Only Live Once) philosophy trumps financial willpower nearly every time when we convince ourselves that "I deserve it" or "I should buy it now since it's such a great deal." Buying that shiny new car creates a euphoric feeling today, but we may wake up to a hangover when the first payment comes due.

Plus, any salesperson worth her salt will make you feel good about yourself once you're behind the wheel of that sweet new boat. She'll convince you it's more affordable than you thought, but that "great deal" loses 20 to 30 percent of its value the minute it's off the lot. Through intensive, time-consuming online research we turn ourselves into experts about the boat we want to purchase, yet we spend only thirty minutes in the business manager's office and rely on him to set us up with financing.

Replacing our bad financial habits with better habits to correct our "disobedient" behavior comes down to discipline. That is, we must learn to control our emotions when making decisions about money. We must learn to build the right habits. Habit science and the emerging field of behavioral finance can help.

We'll cover habits more in Chapter 5.

Following a Financial Plan. We can be financially literate and have reasonably good purchasing habits, but to truly become financially secure, we must prioritize our actions to that end. Having a solid financial future requires not only that we save money but also that we put it to work in the right places and in the correct order.

Building security and wealth is like building a pyramid from the ground up. There are several foundational blocks that should be laid before we move up the pyramid. The middle blocks can get us working towards the future with funds earmarked for family goals. And as we approach the top of the pyramid, investments for the long term become our key building blocks.

In Chapter 6, we'll look at the Wealth Pyramid in detail.

Wherever you start and whatever income you have, developing financial discipline can help you improve your financial position.

ARE YOU READY TO GET BETTER WITH MONEY?

Personal financial success requires a commitment to personal responsibility. Once we are committed to increasing our proficiency with money matters, our knowledge expands quickly and we yearn to increase our learning further. We can then build up our confidence level, which leads to even better financial decisions.

In business, we have a saying: We need to spend time working *on* the business, not just *in* the business. That is, a computer-repair shop owner cannot spend all their time fixing and selling computers (working *in* the business). They must also plan for the future, assess the efficiency of their systems and processes, and think about succession planning (working *on* the business). They need to see the forest as well as the trees.

The same principle applies to our financial health. Rather than staying caught up in our daily routines, personal financial planning requires stepping back to reflect on our longer-term goals. And being able to think critically about our financial goals won't happen until we start asking questions like "Wait, what the heck am I doing?" and "What are my life goals? What is my plan?" and "Should I hire a financial planner, or should I do it myself?"

This book affords you a chance to step back and organize your thoughts on where your money goes. I hope it helps guide you to the promised land of being "good with money." For the readers who commit to at least *some* of the concepts, the book offers a tremendous ROI for the price. None of this stuff is complicated, and it's there for the taking for those who commit to change for the betterment of their financial well-being and security for their families.

Personal finance is all about developing the good habits and patience to take the long road. Unfortunately, in America at least, that tends to be "the road less traveled," to quote Robert Frost. But I can assure you—taking the long road will make all the difference.

CHAPTER 2

OUR COMPLICATED RELATIONSHIP WITH MONEY

SPENDING MONEY TO SHOW PEOPLE HOW
MUCH MONEY YOU HAVE IS THE FASTEST
WAY TO HAVE LESS MONEY.
—MORGAN HOUSEL, *THE PSYCHOLOGY OF MONEY*

LIKE IT OR NOT, we all have a relationship with money. For some of us, it's a warm-fuzzy, long-term relationship. For others, it's a love-hate, on-and-off relationship.

Statistics show that the majority of Americans worry about their personal finances. According to the National Foundation for Credit Counseling (NFCC), 71 percent of Americans report having some sort of money trouble, with "insufficient savings" at the top of the list.[13] The 2019 Mind over Money Survey from Capital One and the Decision Lab found that 77 percent of participants felt anxious about their finances and 58 percent felt that finances controlled their life. Participants in the study found this financial stress caused fatigue (43 percent), difficulty focusing at work (42 percent), and trouble sleeping (41 percent).[14]

We know that we are a nation of spenders relative to most other developed countries, and that our savings rate is on the low end. In 2019 (pre-pandemic), among the approximately forty OECD[15] countries:

- The US ranked third for household spending as a percentage of gross domestic product (GDP), at 67.5%, after Colombia (68.6%) and Greece (69.1%). Compare that to countries at the other end of the spectrum: Ireland at 29.3%, Luxembourg at 33.5%, and China at 39.1%.[16]
- The US ranked fifteenth in household savings as a percentage of household disposable income saved, at 7.9%. Compare that to France at 9.2%, Germany at 10.8%, Mexico at 15.6%, and China at a whopping 34.8%.[17]
- And the US was middle of the pack (18) for household debt as a percentage of net disposable income at 105.4%, with Denmark at the high end at 253.2% and Russia at the low end with 37.4%. (Mexico came in at *negative* 11.5%.)[18]

We have a lot of choices here in the US, with many ways to spend down our incomes and go into debt, but that euphoric feeling you get while shopping may come back to haunt you when the economy tanks and all the bills come due. And with the advent of the modern credit society, it's impossible to know if the neighbors next door can pay all their bills, or whether the next recession will wipe them out. (The old saying is that a recession is when your neighbor loses her job, but a depression is when you lose yours.)

We live in a society that, right or wrong, considers it taboo to discuss salaries (and money in general), so we are left to make educated guesses based on visible clues. We can see our neighbors' shiny new car and big house, but unless there is a tax lien published in the local paper, we have no idea how it was paid for—whether they own it, or the bank does. We essentially assume that a rational person is responsible with money and is in control of their personal finances—in other words, they wouldn't buy a car or house they couldn't afford. But the pressures to buy mount up, even if the executive side of the brain says, "Don't do it—you can't afford it."

In addition, as if figuring out our own equilibrium with money wasn't difficult enough, we're also on a tightrope with our spouse and children and *their* relationships with money. Invariably, arguments over money are at least one of the factors in a divorce. Nearly half (48 percent) of Americans in a marital (or partner) relationship report arguing with their partner over money. And 41 percent of divorced Gen Xers report the split was due to financial issues.[19]

Why do so many of us have a poor relationship with money?

Our spending-related pain is not entirely self-inflicted: there are strong internal and external forces shaping our money decisions consciously and subconsciously, and our view of money is influenced by both nature and nurture. I am a born saver (nature), and my parents and grandparents raised me to practice financial moderation (nurture).

Highlighted next are some of the influential elements of our financial "ecosystem." Once we understand what is influencing us, we can decide whether to let that continue, or to make some changes, because ultimately, the freedom to select our course of action lies within.

OUR FAMILY

Brandon Copeland is not your typical pro football player. He grew up in the Baltimore area with a single mom who instilled discipline in him by not buying him candy bars in the grocery store. The simple lesson of delayed gratification served him well; he first got a college degree from the University of Pennsylvania's Wharton School of Business and *then* got his shot at the NFL (with the Baltimore Ravens) while living at home and driving his mother's secondhand car. Although his father was an unreliable parent, his grandfather, Roy Hilton, was a tremendous role model and inspiration for young Brandon, and kept reminding him that he was one injury away from the finish line of his playing career.

With the average NFL career lasting only three and a half years,[20] Copeland knew how important saving money and investing wisely would be for his long-term well-being. And after realizing that the majority of NFL and NBA players were in financial difficulty within just a few short years of the end of their athletic career, he began saving as much as 90 percent of his income. He discovered that what was most important was finding and honoring what you truly value. Family. Relationships. Opportunities. Sharing.

It is conceivable that many NFL and NBA athletes haven't had the family support and reinforcement that Copeland had. Even if they succeed and earn a large income, the relationship they developed with money growing up may determine whether they can keep any of it once their playing days are finished.

Early experiences with and attitudes from our family of origin are surely some of the most critical influences on our relationship with money. They are also perhaps the most challenging that many of us face. If you grew up in poverty, you may constantly save so that you never experience that feeling of "lack" again; conversely, you may overspend so that you have the material things that make you feel "rich." If you grew up with family members who lived through the Great Depression and learned to save every little scrap of anything that could ever possibly be useful, you may like to travel as light as possible and acquire minimal possessions. If your parents focused on "humility" as a virtue, you may have trouble believing that you deserve a raise or are allowed to have nice things; as a result, you may find yourself underpaid and unable to save. We are all individual in our responses to our family and upbringing, but patterns do arise and you can usually identify early experiences that shaped how you view money.

Later, our choice of marriage or life partner influences us. If both spouses are frugal, it is unlikely there will be a spending problem. However, if he is a spender and she is a saver, it can be difficult to coexist. Her attempts at discussing a budget likely fall on deaf ears; he wants to avoid the conversation and not change his lifestyle, so he opens up a secret credit card. Perhaps it's easiest to go into the marriage agreeing that each will keep their earnings in separate accounts—but then credit becomes an issue unless both commit to paying off their credit card each month.

It can be a tremendous effort, and sometimes require tremendous compromise, to come to an agreement over spending and money management within a marriage. Herein lies the importance of good communication and budgeting. (We'll discuss later why a monthly budget may not be the best answer. When it comes to success rates, I put monthly budgets right up there with diets and New Year's resolutions.) Part of creating a successful marriage comes down to being accountable to each other. I highly suggest pre-marriage counseling, including a discussion of your relationship with money, as a crucial first step in building that relationship.

And I will say this: married or not, if you're the head of your household, you have an obligation to provide for your family. Why would you spend all your money on "stuff" rather than save enough to cover a critical house repair or a copay for your child's medical needs? It makes no sense, does it? Reckless behavior, intentional or not, sacrifices your financial security and well-being. (Okay, getting off my soapbox now.)

PEER PRESSURE

We all remember feeling peer pressure as a kid. Usually it involved doing what our parents asked us *not* to do. For me, it was the fear of missing out ("FOMO" as the kids say today). I never wanted to miss a party or come home early. My friends and I could get into . . . well, let's just say a lot of mischief. The old saying that nothing good happens after midnight was definitely the case. We were lucky to make it home each night, only to rinse and repeat the following night.

Peer pressure keeps coming long after high school is over. In *The* Next *Millionaire Next Door*, Dr. Sarah Stanley Fallaw states that "the neighborhood effect" is a significant influence on our relationship with money. We want to have what our neighbors have, so psychologically we are very much influenced by our neighbors' houses, cars, and possessions. We have all witnessed the neighbor whose kids get the fanciest and most expensive toys at Christmas. "Keeping up with the Joneses" may be the number one spending culprit within all of us. We all (except Ronald Read types) fall for this influence, at least at some level, because we are social creatures. And we all (myself included) enjoy nice things and desire the best for our family.

But there is a built-in status-ladder effect with nearly every purchase out there. Take, for instance, designer clothes. You can go for cheap chic at Target all the way up to shopping on Rodeo Drive with the "beautiful people." Even if we start at the lower end of the ladder, there is pressure on each of us to have nice things based on how society judges us, and we tend to keep climbing up from "necessities" to "wants." When the pressure leads to too many "wants," we can get ourselves in financial trouble. Good common-sense judgment about whether we can afford those designer-label shoes takes a back seat to keeping up with what our peers buy.

As Morgan Housel advised in his book *The Psychology of Money*, "Be nicer and less flashy. No one is impressed with your possessions as much as you are."

THE CONSUMER ECONOMY

It's estimated that in the 1970s, the average American saw 500 to 1,600 ads per day through billboard, newspaper, or TV advertising. In 2007, with product placement and internet advertising added to the mix, that number had grown to 5,000 ads per day. In 2021, some estimates placed the number of ads the average person saw per day between 6,000 and 10,000. Maybe those numbers are excessive and inflated. Okay, let's say we see 1,000 ads per day, or even just 500. That's a helluva lot of advertising.

In addition to family and peer pressure, the other key outside influence on our relationship with money is our consumer economy and the marketing it constantly exposes us to. Our American society is built on consumerism to make the economy grow. How else could we turn a religious holiday into months of advertising that get more intense every year? We spend on this year's Christmas with next year's money. Valentine's Day, Easter, Halloween, birthdays, graduations, weddings, dining out—it all adds up. As I write this, we are beginning to come out of the COVID-19 pandemic and everyone is "ready to get out and enjoy life and spend money," as one person put it— almost as if it's our duty as Americans to spend. Don't fall for this trap. It's your hard-earned money at stake. Let the other gal spend on behalf of the economy.

In addition to the advertising messages we are inundated with, nearly every business out there is collecting at least some data on our buying habits in an attempt to influence our spending. Although we can't eliminate the collection of our purchasing data entirely, it is wise to be aware of and understand the efforts being conducted. The world of "big data" will get even more sophisticated as machine learning and artificial intelligence (AI) become more ubiquitous.

In our current consumer society, we must keep in mind that nearly everyone is trying to sell us something, however subtle their efforts. The key is to recognize this ahead of time so that you can prepare yourself for making solid, conservative decisions and avoid buying on impulse. If we can maintain discipline by avoiding that hasty purchase, then over time we can make more informed and balanced purchasing decisions.

"GET RICH QUICK" MENTALITY

In 1848, gold nuggets were discovered in the Sacramento Valley. Thousands of would-be miners flocked to the area, and by the end of 1849, the non-native population of California had grown from about 1,000 to an estimated 100,000. The allure of a fast fortune and a better way of life was obviously compelling to many who ventured to California upon hearing that the gold was theirs for the taking. But most miners did *not* strike it rich. The ones to prosper from the rush were mainly the merchants—the so-called "pick-and-shovel" salesmen.

America has always had an entrepreneurial spirit about it, as well as a get-rich-quick mentality. This desire for instant gratification has gotten much worse with reality TV stars, online bloggers, and YouTube video sensations grabbing much of the exposure and press in our daily lives. The entrepreneurial spirit of building a traditional business through sweat equity has shifted to a fast-paced online "gold rush." All you need is your YouTube business to get a million hits and you're on Easy Street.

Our want-it-and-gotta-have-it-now society makes it more challenging to build wealth the traditional way—over many years rather than in a few short months. But wealth creation is about saving money and then using time as our advantage. I'm sure it never occurred to Ron Read to change up his lifestyle. In some ways, he sacrificed his own well-being (at least by today's standards) to leave gifts for the greater good of his community. He viewed stock market investing much the same way we enjoy a hobby such as coin collecting. It's likely that he never calculated his full net worth; he just collected those stock certificates and put them aside. His line of thinking was in decades rather than in moments.

Another good example of the get-rich-quick mentality and the external pressure it exerts on us is the lottery. I can't speak for every state, but North Carolina heavily advertises its lottery on television. The allure of exciting new games to play can be enticing for the poorest of our citizens. Winning could solve all their problems. But we all know (or should know) that the chances of being struck by lightning are greater than those of hitting a big jackpot. The lottery becomes one of the worst forms of a regressive tax, since a $20-per-week habit is a *lot* of discretionary weekly income for the lowest wage earners.

Yet we condone the behavior of participating in the lottery as "supporting education." (It's the North Carolina Education Lottery, after all.) While it may be true that lottery funds get some schools built, we are dumbing ourselves down every time we buy a lottery ticket. What we really need is an education system that teaches financial literacy and personal finance (in 2019 North Carolina passed just such a requirement for high school[21]).

The lottery is a great example of peer pressure, advertising, and the get-rich-quick mentality all rolled into one. When our society encourages us to support education by playing the lottery, it's no wonder we struggle with money management decisions.

CONFIRMATION BIAS

Mark Twain is often credited with saying "It ain't what you don't know that gets you in trouble. It's what you know for sure that just ain't so." And ain't that true . . . No matter how impartial we believe ourselves to be, we cannot help but favor information that supports what we already believe or what we *want* to believe to be true. We will favor what fits our narrative. This is what's known as *confirmation bias*.

But often what we *want* to do probably doesn't match up with what we *should* do, insofar as our being able to comfortably afford it. Taking the time to study financial matters, and throwing in a bit of critical thinking, can go a long way towards making solid money decisions. Good first steps are to increase our financial literacy enough that we can comfortably discuss interest rates, the time value of money, and depreciating assets vs. appreciating assets, and to learn rules of thumb that can help keep us financially grounded and solvent. There is more to come on these points in Chapter 4.

OUR OWN CHOICES

Despite all these influences—family, friends, society at large—the ultimate driver of our spending behavior and relationship to money is us. *We* make the executive choices within our brains to spend or not to spend, to save or not to save. *We* create the habits that put us on a track to wealth or debt. *We* get to consider the factors that have influenced us and decide what to change in our relationship with money.

In Chapter 5, we'll look at exchanging poor money habits for healthier ones, but next up, we look at five money personality types that manifest in response to all the influences we've discussed in this chapter.

CHAPTER 3

MONEY PERSONALITY TYPES

DON'T TELL ME WHERE YOUR PRIORITIES ARE.
SHOW ME WHERE YOU SPEND YOUR MONEY
AND I'LL TELL YOU WHAT THEY ARE.
—JAMES W. FRICK, NOTRE DAME UNIVERSITY

As A RESULT OF OUR upbringing and our experiences, we've all developed views and beliefs about money that are so personal they're as unique as our DNA. Everyone has their own style and their own money identity, but we do tend to follow certain patterns.

I've identified five financial personality types: Spendthrifts, Shoppers, Savers, Investors, and Gamblers. A Spendthrift is definitely not a Saver; the two are mutually exclusive. And there are certainly differences between a Spendthrift and a true Shopper. A Shopper *can* be a Saver (or not). As we will see, a Saver may well be an Investor but then again may not be. An Investor likely is a Saver first. And finally, a Gambler is the get-rich-quick type whose vocabulary does not include the word patience. So, got all that?

Well, enough. Let's take a look . . .

SPENDTHRIFTS

The etymology of the word *spendthrift* is interesting. Today it's considered an oxymoronic word—that is, it's made up of two words with seemingly opposite connotations. *Spend* means "to use up or pay out." *Thrift* means "careful management especially of money." So when you put them together, does it mean you spend a lot, or save a lot?

One of the older meanings of *thrift* is "savings." So a *spendthrift* is someone who is spending their savings. Or, as Merriam-Webster defines it, "a person who spends improvidently or wastefully." (Interesting enough, a synonym from *way* back in the day was *dingthrift*, with *ding* meaning "to deal a heavy blow"—so a dingthrift basically pulverizes their savings.)

We all know the Spendthrift type: they're the person who, if they won the lottery, would spend all the money in a few short years. They go through their money as quick as they can. Fine clothing, jewelry, furniture, and luxury car salespeople love these folks. The impulse to spend on the finest "stuff" is just too great to overcome. When the euphoria of that new clothing wears off, they move to the next impulse purchase to keep the habit going. And maxing out the credit cards . . . these folks don't care about the cost. Their mentality is "only the best will do"—and that goes double if their child is involved. Frugality is just not in their DNA.

Perhaps they came from a meager upbringing that shaped their emotions as a child and have swung the pendulum the opposite direction. They may also be the type that has a real zest for living, with many expensive hobbies. The latest golf, hunting, and fishing equipment can add up fast, and when one or two shotguns would suffice, the Spendthrift collects a dozen or more.

Spendthrifts may have a few pet areas of weakness, but my view is that they seem to be always on the go and ready for their next adventure. They are often personable and fun to be around since they have the finer things to enjoy. They let you know (sometimes without your asking) how great their latest trip was and that you just *have* to go on that cruise. For them, Facebook posts are an opportunity to share photos of their new car or remodeled kitchen. (I quit Facebook years ago when I could no longer tolerate folks bragging about the latest restaurant they had discovered and posting pictures of dinner plates. I was already satisfied with my Myspace account. LOL.)

It is tempting to admire the Spendthrift since they seem to have it all together. You wonder how they can possibly pay for it all, which may lead you to feel insecure about your own possessions. But if both spouses are Spendthrifts and neither is responsible with the household budget, then financial counseling may be in order, or else divorce may threaten.

SHOPPERS

Next are the Shoppers, whose mission in life is to secure the best deal ever. They love the hunt. They cut store coupons and keep a wallet full of store credit cards. They lose sleep knowing they overpaid for an item, and they'll drive all over town to save $20. They can't wait to tell their friends what expertise they're employing as they look for their next conquest. They always know where to locate the best bargains, and they spend much of their time in pursuit of a deal. The Shopper may possess frugality in their spending patterns, but it appears they do enjoy spending since they always seem to be shopping for something—and it doesn't really matter what that something is.

Suffice it to say that neither the Spendthrift nor the Shopper is very good on the saving and investing side of the financial equation. A Shopper may save fairly well inside a household budget, but most are not skilled at where the money should be parked and invested—they are too busy "saving" money as a professional shopper by taking advantage of every store discount they can get their hands on. The Shopper brags about getting something for 40 percent off, yet how much useless stuff have they accumulated? The thought of having to pay twelve different store credit cards plus Visa every month never occurs to them since their motivation is saving money. "Time is money" means little to Shoppers. "Fun" for them is going to Target at 4:00 a.m. on Black Friday!

SAVERS

A lot of folks *are* frugal and do an excellent job tucking away their money. These are the Savers. Savers likely do not shop much, and they are good at saving their money *before* considering a significant purchase. Savers are usually financially comfortable and in a good position whenever an emergency expense arrives. Most Savers are just not motivated to have a lot of "stuff." They are often minimalists who believe in the creed "Live life simply"—and the most effective way to live life simply is to keep their lives clutter-free. Why do I need twenty-five pairs of shoes when I can wear only one or two pairs per day?

Savers are comfortable not buying a car new—or even worrying about what kind of car they drive in the first place. Keeping a budget is never an issue for them because they are going to be careful with each dollar to begin with. Savers may have had parents and grandparents from the Great Depression and World War II eras who repeated stories ad nauseam about having very little. My mother tells the story of the sugar rations during WWII. She recalls when she was eleven years old, she came home from grocery shopping with my grandmother and dropped the bag of sugar on the front doorstep. It burst. No matter: she gathered it up to save nearly every bit of her ration.

Because Savers tend to be a cautious and risk-averse lot, they are often not adept at investing. They don't trust the stock market and have no use for Wall Street. They prefer a savings account, maybe a certificate of deposit (CD), and they will max their 401(k) contribution as a form of payroll savings. They are doing okay but are just not willing to take the next step. Keeping their money safe is more critical than risking any principal. The thought of losing their principal brings on much stronger emotions than making a great investment ever will. They may even understand the concepts of inflation and compound interest, but keeping their money in front of them where they can see it is a bigger priority. If Savers could get to a more comfortable place with the concepts of investing, they could move up to be an Investor. The key is gaining the confidence to take on some added risk.

INVESTORS

The next group is the Investors, who are financially literate and understand how wealth is built. They share a lot of characteristics with Savers; however, they are likely more sophisticated and understand risk a bit better than Savers do. Savers are great at having money in the bank but may not understand macroeconomics, including the risk inflation poses to their future purchasing power and real rate of return. A conservative Investor understands the importance of earning a return on their money that keeps up with the rate of inflation. A more astute and sophisticated Investor comprehends compound interest and how to build wealth over time. This "intelligent investor," as the late economist Benjamin Graham put it, understands the risks of *not* having an appropriate investing strategy to reach their financial goals. In other words, they know there is just as much risk in not earning a positive return above inflation as there is in potentially losing principal.

However, Investors can be fairly risk averse with their hard-earned savings and may hold too much debt. In many instances they are focused on their investment returns being greater than their debt borrowing rates. For example, they could be reluctant to pay down a mortgage with an interest rate of 5% when they are earning double that in the market. However, it could be advisable to pay down some debt and keep investing concurrently. We'll cover more on this later.

GAMBLERS

Gamblers live life on the edge—or at least in the fast lane. The chance to hit it big with their investments is what motivates them. They are impatient, and many seem to have characteristics of attention deficit hyperactivity disorder (ADHD). Saving for retirement is boring and works too slowly. Gamblers are the stock speculators and day traders; long-term investments simply will not keep their attention. They follow the market's every gyration and are intrigued whenever something like cryptocurrency comes along to strike their fancy.

Gamblers may share traits with the Spendthrift; they often view their short-term trading as a way to keep their spending habits going—after all, they are sure to get quick wins with windfall profits. They are also impressionable and may be envious if they have a friend who makes money on risky investments while they miss out. Gamblers love the thrill of staying at the table with the best. In the movie *Rounders*, Matt Damon's character's main goal in life is to be good enough to sit in at the poker table with Johnny Chan (a real-life professional poker player). Knowing that he was good enough "that one time" to hang with the professional gambler motivates him to pursue his own professional gambling career. Just like surfer Bodhi in the cult classic movie *Point Break*, Gamblers seem to be always searching for the "ultimate ride."

SUMMARY OF MONEY PERSONALITIES

	SPENDTHRIFT	SHOPPER	SAVER	INVESTOR	GAMBLER
SPENDING BEHAVIOR	Spends lavishly without concern for the future	Spends frequently; always looks for a "deal"	Spends only on what is needed; saves up for big purchases	Spends like a Saver; as wealth grows, spending may grow	May or may not spend a lot
SAVING BEHAVIOR	Minimal saving, if any	May have some savings	Saves regularly	Saves and has a large cushion for emergencies	Typically doesn't save much
INVESTING BEHAVIOR	Minimal investing, if any	Minimal investing, if any	Makes low-risk investments (CDs, index funds); contributes to 401(k), avoids "risky" stocks	Has solid foundation in 401(k) and mutual funds; beats inflation by investing in stocks for the long haul	Day-trades or tries to time the market; looks for short-term wins
ADVICE	Spend less; save more	Question motives for shopping; save more	Keep saving; increase financial literacy and begin investing	Keep on keepin' on!	Learn patience; start investing at least some money for the long term

WHAT IS YOUR MONEY PERSONALITY?

Thinking back to some of the personalities we began the book with, what profile(s) do you think Ronald Read fits? Saver and Investor, obviously. How about Boris Becker? Spendthrift perhaps, and maybe Gambler. Hunt Hartford was certainly a Spendthrift. And Barbara Corcoran is clearly an Investor.

Do you recognize yourself in one of the five money personalities? Do you like what you see in the mirror? Or do you need to make some changes? I advise almost everyone to shoot for the Investor profile, but changes aren't made overnight so begin slowly if you need to.

If you are a Spendthrift, your first step may be to target some of the Shopper's behaviors and at least become more frugal in your spending. The Shopper may need to take on more of the Saver's characteristics and think twice about what they are buying and why they are buying it. The Saver is in a strong position, and if that's you, congratulations. Your next step is to increase your financial literacy and learn to take on risk that can improve your financial position in the long run. If you are a Gambler, well, you're probably not reading this book, but I'd recommend acquiring some Saver and Investor traits—learn patience. If you are already an Investor, congratulations—you probably aren't reading this book either, because you've got things covered, but if you are, there's always room to increase your financial literacy and improve your investing decisions, so don't stop learning.

Additionally, if you have a spouse or partner, consider their money personality. How does it affect your relationship? Do you have joint accounts and joint credit cards? Or do you keep your money and your accounts separate? Or is it a hybrid of the two? Does one of you get stuck with all of the household expenses while the other gets all of the "fun money"? Does understanding your money personality shed some light on conflicts in your relationship?

Maybe you're not yet convinced you need to make a change. Or maybe you need more information to feel comfortable making changes. The more you know, the clearer it becomes what you need to do, so let's take a look at financial literacy next.

PART TWO

BUILDING FINANCIAL
DISCIPLINE

IN PART ONE, you got an idea of life experiences that may have influenced your relationship with money, what your resulting money personality is, and whether you have room to improve your financial security through greater financial discipline.

In Part Two, we look at the three components of financial discipline: gaining financial literacy, managing our money habits, and following a financial plan. These are all things that are learnable and doable over time. You don't have to do everything at once, and I encourage you to begin taking small steps and making incremental changes even as you read this book.

CHAPTER 4

FINANCIAL LITERACY

A NICKEL AIN'T WORTH A DIME ANYMORE.

—YOGI BERRA

ANSWER THESE QUICK QUESTIONS about investing and personal finance:[22]

1. Suppose you had $100 in a savings account and the interest rate was 2% per year. After five years, how much do you think you would have in the account if you left the money to grow?
   A. More than $102
   B. Exactly $102
   C. Less than $102
   D. Don't know

2. Imagine that the interest rate on your savings account was 1% per year and inflation was 2% per year. After one year, how much would you be able to buy with the money in this account?

A. More than today
B. Exactly the same as today
C. Less than today
D. Don't know

3. Buying a single company's stock usually provides a safer return than a stock mutual fund.
A. True
B. False
C. Don't know

How did you do on the quiz? See the answers at the end of the chapter.

This quiz, now known as the "Big Three," was developed by Annamaria Lusardi and Olivia S. Mitchell of the Wharton School, the University of Pennsylvania's business school. It has become a financial literacy standard worldwide. Only 30 percent of Americans can answer all three questions correctly.

(Visitors to Lusardi's website, www.annamarialusardi.com/research/projects/, are directed to take the original version of the test on the website of the Global Financial Literacy Excellence Center at https://gflec.org/education/big-three/.)

In my experience, people often think they know more than they actually do, and in the absence of a financial education, their "common sense" can get them in trouble. In fact, a survey by the National Financial Educators Council (NFEC) found that in 2021 financial illiteracy cost Americans an average of $1,389 per person, which, generalized to 254 million adults, means lack of financial literacy cost us a total of more than $352 billion.[23] So maybe you can see why I'm so concerned about financial literacy and why I want to see us improve.

When personal computers came about in the 1990s, the computer geeks introduced us to an entirely new lexicon—DOS, GUI, mouse, server, operating system, .com, cookies, floppy disk, thumb drive—that we had to learn and keep learning in order to be efficient in our jobs. Similarly, to meet our financial goals, we must build financial discipline, and the first step in that is to build our financial vocabulary and increase our financial literacy.

KEY FINANCIAL CONCEPTS

To begin or continue your financial education, here are the financial concepts I believe are necessary to know and understand before you can reach your financial goals. These principles are key to moving from a "common sense" worldview to a more disciplined financial approach and to making personal financial decisions that are in your and your family's best interests.

CASH FLOW

Cash flow is simply money coming in and money going out. If your income "flowing in" can cover all of your expenses, then you have a *positive cash flow*. If your expenses "flowing out" are higher than your income flowing in, that means you are funding the gap with debt and have *negative cash flow*. Making sure your cash flow is positive is a key starting point when setting your personal budget. (More on budgeting in Chapter 5.)

ASSETS AND LIQUIDITY

An *asset* is anything with present or future value, and it may lose value (*depreciate*) or gain value (*appreciate*). Common examples of *personal assets* include cash, checking and savings accounts, real estate and structures attached to it (like your house), personal property (such as cars and household furnishings), and investments (such as stocks, mutual funds, retirement plans, and bonds).

Assets have varying degrees of *liquidity*. An asset that is liquid can be converted to cash quickly. (By "cash" we mean bank deposits, not cash buried in the backyard!) For example, cash itself is always the most liquid asset, and mutual funds and stocks are fairly liquid, whereas raw (undeveloped) land is illiquid, as it takes time to sell and, depending on the market, may not sell at all.

INVESTMENT

An *investment* is an asset that has the potential to and is expected to increase in value over time; common examples include stocks and mutual funds. Some investments may also contribute to our return on investment (ROI) through payment of interest or dividends. Income-producing assets such as rental properties are investments as well.

Your investment options are nearly unlimited, ranging from certificates of deposit to mutual funds to commodities like gold and silver. We'll cover investments in more detail in Chapter 7.

LIABILITIES, DEBT, AND LEVERAGE

A *liability* is something you owe; that is, it is a *debt*. Your mortgage is a liability, your monthly credit card balance is a liability, your student loan is a liability. Anything that has to be paid for at some point in the future is a liability.

A mortgage is a form of *installment loan*, in which a set amount of money is borrowed with a set repayment schedule. Credit cards, by contrast, are the most popular form of *revolving credit*, a form of credit that lets you repeatedly borrow up to a certain dollar amount. Another common form of revolving credit is a home equity line of credit, or HELOC. Running up a balance on a credit card is the worst kind of debt (other than a loan shark!), since the interest is compounded daily on the average of your monthly balance using a high interest rate, typically 12% to 18%.

When you take on debt to purchase something, you are using a concept called *leverage*. You are increasing your purchasing power through utilizing debt, but leverage creates risk that could put you into trouble when the next recession arrives and you struggle to make the payments on the debt. The digital credit-card world makes it easier than ever to spend with debt, so it becomes critical to watch your cash flow and follow a balanced budget.

NET WORTH

Net worth is a measurement of wealth. It is the value of assets owned minus liabilities owed. If you have $100k in assets and owe $25k, your net worth is $75k. (The letter "k" is short for thousand.) Net worth should not be confused with income. You may have a high income, but if you spend it all, you may have a low or even negative net worth.

Building net worth takes time and patience, but having a solid net worth means you have some money in reserve for when times get difficult. Additionally, having that financial cushion gives you easier access to loans such as mortgages, because it provides lenders some confidence that you have a secondary source of loan repayment should something happen to your day job.

PERSONAL FINANCIAL STATEMENT

A *personal financial statement*, or *PFS*, is simply a list of your assets and liabilities that shows your net worth. (A PFS is comparable to a *balance sheet* for a business.) The assets are typically listed by liquidity, with the most liquid first and the least liquid (most illiquid) last. A PFS is a useful tool for monitoring your financial status, but it is also used—and scrutinized—when you apply for loans, such as mortgages. The more debt you accumulate, the more leveraged your PFS becomes, which may cause the bank to view you as a higher risk and thus charge you higher loan interest rates.

RATE OF RETURN AND REAL RATE OF RETURN

Rate of return is the net gain or loss on an investment over a period of time, often a year, expressed as a percentage. If we invest $100 for a year and earn $3, we have a rate of return of 3%.

Real rate of return is what we earn on an investment adjusted for inflation. If we keep all of our investments in a money market account earning 0.3% and inflation is 3% (according to the Consumer Price Index, or CPI), our rate of return would be 0.3%, but our *real* rate of return would be –2.7%. This is because the annual rate of inflation at 3% is far greater than the measly 0.3% we are earning on our savings, which means we are losing buying power (2.7% worth) every year.

Real rate of return is important, because if we don't at least keep up with the rate of inflation, our buying power shrinks over time. In other words, if the annual rate of inflation is 3%, then we must earn at least 3% on our savings and investments to keep our buying power unchanged. (If you are a Saver who has yet to invest in the stock market, chances are you are losing buying power by leaving your money in savings, CDs, and low-yield bonds.)

Over the past century, the inflation rate in the US has averaged just over 3% but has ranged from almost –16% (deflation) to almost 24%.[24] Inflation has been fairly low for the first two decades of the twenty-first century, but around the COVID-19 pandemic it started becoming a real issue again, with rates unlike anything seen since the 1980s.

If you take nothing else away from this book, remember that unless your rate of return beats inflation, you are losing buying power over time.

COMPOUND INTEREST AND THE RULE OF 72

When you take out a loan, the loan amount is your *principal*. You pay interest on the principal. If you pay interest only on the original principal amount, that is called *simple interest*. Many automobile loans and mortgages charge simple interest. With credit cards, however, you pay interest on both the principal and on any accumulated interest; this is called *compound interest*. Likewise, when you have an investment, the amount invested is your principal, and compound interest is the interest calculated on the principal and interest already earned. Think of compound interest as interest on interest. Compound interest lets your original investment amount grow faster than simple interest would.

For example, if I invest $100 and earn simple interest of 10% each year, I would get $10 each year (10% × $100 = $10). If I invest the same amount but get compound interest, I would get $10 in interest the first year (same calculation), but I would get $11 the second year because the calculation is now 10% × $110 = $11. The following year, the calculation would be 10% × $121 = $12.10, so after three years I have $133.10, whereas with simple interest I would have only $130. This might not sound like a lot when we are talking about $100, but add a couple zeroes and a significant amount of time, and we're talking about a material difference.

Calculating compound interest can feel like a math headache, so the *Rule of 72* is a handy shortcut that can be useful when setting your financial goals. Here's how it works: To determine how many years it will take to double your money, divide 72 by the annual rate of return. So if we keep our money in that savings account earning only 0.3% compounded annually, we can expect our money to double in 240 years (72 ÷ 0.3 = 240).

By contrast, if we are able to earn 7.2% on our savings (a reasonable stock market return), we can double our money in ten years ($72 \div 7.2 = 10$). If inflation stays at around 3% per year on average, our buying power also increases by 4.2% (7.2% – 3.0% = 4.2%).

If we invested $10,000 today, earning 7.2%, the Rule of 72 tells us our money would grow to $80,000 in thirty years (our money doubles every ten years, so $10k × 2 = $20k; $20k × 2 = $40k; $40k × 2 = $80k). Our savings account making 0.3%? We'd need another 690 years *beyond* those thirty years to reach $80,000.

AMORTIZATION

Amortization describes how loan payments get applied to principal and interest each month over the life of a loan. For example, let's say you take out a simple $300,000, 5% fixed-rate mortgage with a 30-year amortization (5% might sound high if you were lucky enough to buy at 2% or 3%, but it is actually historically low). Each monthly payment you make (in this case around $1,610) pays back some principal and pays for some interest. When you start out making payments, the interest is usually the larger part of the payment and the principal is the smaller. Over time, as you pay down the principal, the ratio changes and the amount going towards principal increases. After ten years, you'll have paid about $56,600 in principal and $138,300 in interest. You will still owe about $243,400 on your mortgage, thus your *equity* (the value of the portion you own) is $56,600 (assuming the house did not appreciate or depreciate).

If instead you choose a 15-year amortization, the payments are more each month ($2,372), but the extra money pays down your loan faster, in half the time. After ten years, you'll have paid about $176,100 in principal and $110,900 in interest, and the remaining balance will be only $123,900 compared to the $243,400 for the 30-year. You will now have equity of $176,100 compared to only $56,600 with the 30-year amortization—three times more! (Again, we did not factor in any appreciation or depreciation on the market value of the house.)

Suffice it to say that if you move four times and always choose the 30-year amortization, you'll never build up any equity from your home "ownership" and you'll be paying a mortgage until you're eighty. This is why I recommend a 15-year mortgage if you want to use your house to build equity (and thus wealth) over time.

Want to see for yourself the impact of these factors? Just go online and search for "amortization calculators." Input various loan amounts, loan periods, and interest rates to see how your total cost changes as the factors change.

OPPORTUNITY COSTS IN FINANCIAL DECISIONS

There are only twenty-four hours in the day. If you choose to spend eight hours working, those are eight hours where you give up the opportunity to sleep or read or spend time with your family. The thing you *didn't* do is called your *opportunity cost*.

Money also comes with opportunity costs. For $20, you can buy a book, or you can buy five cups of coffee for yourself and your pals. Whichever one you don't buy is your opportunity cost. You are constantly making these trade-offs, even if you don't realize it.

Let's say you need to decide whether to use your money to pay down debt or to put it in an investment account for retirement. Do you choose the Dave Ramsey, all-in, aggressive debt-reduction plan and miss out on stock market returns? Or do you make only the scheduled payments on the house and put everything else into the market? It likely depends on your mortgage rate and how the market is performing.

Say your mortgage rate is 4%. If you assume the market will make the 7.2% return we mentioned earlier (which is not an unreasonable assumption in the long term), then you can make more money by investing (7.2%) than you can by paying down your debt (4%). Paying down debt means we are giving up the market's potential upside—that is our opportunity cost.

But what if the market is flat or stocks are falling and you can't project market gains with any confidence? Assume you would make 0% by investing in the market. Paying down your debt would, in effect, earn you 4%—better than the market. So if you still choose to invest in the market when it is flat/declining, your opportunity cost is the 4% you could "earn" by paying down debt.

It is important to always compare your investment earnings to your cost of credit. For example, you wouldn't want to carry credit card debt at 18% in order to invest in the market that is returning 7%. And it may be smart to both pay down debt *and* invest. These are good "dilemmas" to have since they indicate you're in the analytical stage of financial decision-making.

Additionally, I will say that opportunity cost is not entirely financial. Debt carries emotional weight as well. So even if the numbers say, "Sure, hang onto that low-cost loan because you can make more money elsewhere," you may feel happier eliminating all but the most essential debt. Your mental and emotional health are an intangible opportunity cost to account for in your financial decision-making.

STOCKS VS. BONDS

We'll cover investments in Chapter 7, but it's important to understand the difference between stocks and bonds.

Stocks represent equity, or ownership, in a company. When you buy a stock, you are referred to as an *investor*, although you actually become one of sometimes many "owners" of the company. (You are a real owner, but chances are you aren't a *hands-on* owner of the company.) When you hear about "the stock market," normally this refers to common stocks sold on a public exchange such as the NYSE (New York Stock Exchange) or the NASDAQ (the National Association of Securities Dealers Automated Quotations).

The primary reason to buy a stock is so you can participate in the future earnings of the company. As an owner, you have the prospect of your shares gaining in value (or *appreciating*) over time. Additionally, some companies make payments, called *dividends*, to shareholders, typically on a quarterly basis. These two facets of stock ownership—appreciation and regular dividend payments—are sometimes referred to as *growth* and *income*, and investors often choose individual stocks with one or the other in mind. What we mean by *total return* is the combination of the two.

Bonds, on the other hand, represent debt for the company. When you buy a bond, you are essentially giving the company a long-term loan in return for interest payments, known as *coupon payments*, typically made twice a year. On the end date, the bonds *mature* and the principal becomes due (that is, you are paid back the original money you loaned the company).

Bonds can be bought and sold prior to maturity, which means they have not only their intrinsic value (the value of the coupon payments) but also a market price. Say a bond pays 5%. If a newer bond comes out that pays 6%, the market price of the 5% bond will go down, because the 6% bond is more attractive. If, on the other hand, the interest paid by the new bond is only 4%, then the 5% bond becomes more attractive and its market price goes up. Thus we can say that bond prices have an inverse relationship to interest rates. Note that this movement changes only the price, not the intrinsic value. (If you are holding individual bonds to maturity, you are not losing money.) However, this relationship is worth understanding, because many people have a portfolio of bonds somewhere in their 401(k) plan, so changes in interest rates will affect its performance.

Because stock investors are partial owners of the company, they take on more risk than bond holders do, because debt holders always get paid before owners do. So, for example, if the company goes bankrupt, there is a "seniority" among creditors, with the most "senior" claims (i.e., the strongest claims, such as those backed by collateral) getting paid first. Thus senior secured creditors, such as banks and bond holders, are first in line to get paid. The stock owners are always last in line because they *own* the company; in essence, the debt is theirs to pay. Put another way, stockholders don't have a claim to anything except profit—*if* there is any profit left after the debts are paid.

RESOURCES FOR INCREASING YOUR FINANCIAL LITERACY

When I was young, I enjoyed picking up *Reader's Digest* and reading "It Pays to Increase Your Word Power," which was basically a vocabulary quiz. It always made me feel like I was a bit dense, but I would recommend a similar "quiz" strategy to increase your financial knowledge of money matters. Take a half hour or so at night (in between important activities like binge-watching the Kardashians) to study a financial topic that interests you or can help with a money decision. I can guarantee you'll learn something. In the appendix, I provide some good resources to start with, including recommended books and several online resources. As you begin learning, keep in mind two key points . . .

First, look for unbiased sources, which may be trickier to find than you think. You must constantly consider the motive behind what you are reading, to make sure it is relevant to what is needed and not just another sales pitch. Pitches are everywhere and can be subtle. For example, I recently picked up a copy of an investment magazine. The magazine cover was promoting a feature article inside on the merits of annuities, but when you turned to the article itself, you found it was actually an advertisement for an annuity company that had paid for a cover wrap around the magazine. Once you removed the wrap, you could see the magazine's real cover.

Why is this significant? The magazine's core subscribers are registered investment advisors (RIAs), who as fiduciaries are bound to act in their clients' best interests. The magazine should be providing its RIA readers clear and unbiased articles and advice. To "trick" readers by using a slick wrapper ad is bad enough, but the product in this case happened to be annuities, which are (or should be) controversial products for RIAs to sell due to their infamously high fees. The integrity of the magazine suffers from this decision to use misleading messaging.

Second, when it comes to your money and key financial decisions, it pays to rely on more than one source. The worst possible single source is *us*, due to the internal conflicts of interest we create for ourselves. We know what we want to have happen, and cognitive bias is simply too strong an emotional pull in our brains. So we must do our homework. The idea of *triangulation* is that we use at least three sources to increase our odds of making a solid decision. By considering multiple sources, we can greatly reduce our chance of making an uninformed decision and can lead ourselves to a more rational and thoughtful choice.

For example, if you're interested in investing in Bitcoin, you could join an online group that can advise you along the way. Maybe your next-door neighbor is a math professor who can explain how cryptocurrency works. And perhaps you can consult with a financial advisor who has some experience in how to invest in cryptocurrencies while also mitigating the risk. At least if you take the time to gather data using a minimum of three sources, you have a better chance of success.

■■■

I believe understanding key financial concepts is one of the crucial steps to making great money decisions. Another important step is to develop good money habits to go along with your financial knowledge. In the next chapter, we'll discuss common mistakes most of us make at some point as well as better habits that can give us an edge.

(Quiz Answers: 1-A, 2-C, 3-B.)

CHAPTER 5

MANAGING YOUR MONEY HABITS

ONCE YOU UNDERSTAND THAT HABITS CAN
CHANGE, YOU HAVE THE FREEDOM—AND THE
RESPONSIBILITY—TO REMAKE THEM.
—CHARLES DUHIGG, *THE POWER OF HABIT*

IT SEEMS THAT WHEN it comes to money there are more ways to make bad decisions than good ones. Perhaps this explains why most of us struggle with money matters—spending is easy and fun, and saving is slow and unexciting. However, I am convinced that many of our bad decisions are due to poor habits, so the second component of developing financial discipline is learning to change our poor money habits into good ones. This involves managing our emotions, which, as you know, isn't always easy, but it is worth it.

One of the best books I've read in recent years is *The Power of Habit* by Charles Duhigg. Duhigg stresses throughout the book that humans are like Pavlov's dog in that we act on stimulus. That is, we all get into repetitive cycles of habit, which can be our downfall when it comes to spending. According to Duhigg, the key is to replace our bad habits with good ones. For example, if you can replace that morning Starbucks habit with making coffee at home, that can save you an easy $1,000 annually right there.

In his book, Duhigg describes the habit "loop" as a cue, a routine, and a reward. The cue kicks off the routine, and the reward reinforces it. The loop continues to the point that the routine repeats without our being conscious of it. Our willpower to adjust the routine becomes weaker and weaker until we realize the routine has solidified into a habit. We all have and develop habits in our daily lives, such as getting ready for work every morning before heading out: the alarm clock is the *cue* that it's time to get up, the *routine* is dressing, showering, and so on to get ready, and the *reward* is getting to work on time. The cue of having to get up doesn't change. The reward of getting to work on time doesn't change; that is, *if you are on time*, you get the reward. The problem is when you are *not* on time. The variable piece, which determines whether we are on time, is the routine between cue and reward that repeats each day as our habit loop. So, if we are habitually late to work, we must change or speed up our morning routine to get to work on time.

The ability to make adjustments to our daily routine is the titular power of habit we desire. But making those adjustments—changing those habits—can be difficult. There's an old saying: "Willpower is always on will-call." Not true. We have a limited supply of willpower and can't just summon it up whenever we want to make changes. It takes work to think through why we fall into the bad habits that we do.

How can we use this habit-loop process in our daily financial lives? Routines are part of life, so they can't be avoided (nor should they be), but they can be adjusted. Back to Duhigg's key: replacing the bad habit with a better one. If we know we need to get in the habit of saving money, we must address our routine so we think differently about where our money goes during a week, then a month, then a year. This savings example is analogous to the old Weight Watchers (now WW) system of dieting: counting calories. To have success in saving more money, we first must be willing to see where it all goes. Whether you track your expenses with pen and paper or in an Excel spreadsheet makes no difference, as long as you create "aha moments" by identifying wasteful spending—and we all (except maybe Ronald Read) waste at least some money. By cutting out the daily Starbucks run or the weekly routine of buying a lottery ticket, we can adjust the routine to reap the reward, such as putting an additional $300 a month in our savings account. (I know Starbucks is a trite example, but I bet you have one of these Starbucks-type habits in your life—what is it?) Otherwise, we go through life like Charlie Harper on *Two and a Half Men*—he never wants to change his lifestyle but wonders why he's out of money!

It comes down to thinking, "Where is my money going, and how can I change my routine?" The wealth that can result from saving more and spending less is the ultimate reward, but it takes willpower to change the habits in our daily routine to achieve our goals. Let's look first at some of the most common poor money habits so you can see what patterns you may want to adjust, and then we'll look at the three key habits wealthy people tend to have.

POOR MONEY HABITS (WHAT NOT TO DO)

By identifying poor money habits, we can be successful in saving more money simply by avoiding bad choices. As mentioned in Chapter 2, the deck is stacked against us with the aforementioned societal pressure to spend, usually on items not in our long-term best interests, but ultimately, *we* have the control. Here are six bad habits many Americans have.

BAD HABIT #1: BUYING FROM CONVENIENCE

We all spend money, and plenty of it, on convenience: food deliveries, drive-through services, and Amazon next-day service. (We haven't always had a pandemic as an excuse, and hopefully we won't in the future either.) All businesses must make a profit, and they charge a premium for convenience.

Observe the purchasing patterns at the local convenience store. We all know that the gas pump outside (with the obnoxious video screen) is only the "draw" to get you inside. Once you're there, your goose is cooked. There are no bargains in a c-store. Common grocery items are priced higher than they would be at a grocery store, and items that are prominently featured, such as lottery tickets, beer, cigarettes, and snacks, can consume a high percentage of disposable income, especially for those with lower incomes. Additionally, many of these items are taxed heavily, resulting in a regressive form of tax.

This "convenient" world order we have created is having a detrimental effect on our health as well as our spending habits, with convenience (which often means "laziness") bringing obesity to epidemic proportions. It reminds me of the Carousel of Progress at Walt Disney World. We've "progressed" from having to hunt for our food to pushing a few buttons and having our dinner brought right to our door. We are past the point where convenience is improving our lives. Our "too much of a good thing" has led to laziness and complacency, when more effort would lead to a more positive outcome.

Convenience has its place, but the watch-out is to monitor the time saved against the related spending as well as the impact on our well-being. It takes discipline to avoid taking too many convenient shortcuts.

Pro tip: Track your spending for a week to see where it goes. Identify what is a need versus a habit of convenience.

BAD HABIT #2: EATING OUT EXCESSIVELY

The next big mistake a lot of us make is eating out too much. Part of the blame here goes to convenience and part of it to the Joneses effect—we all love to eat out with a group of friends as a social thing. Plus, if you live in a decent-sized town, there is always a new restaurant to try. Especially for the young and the recently married, it is tempting to eat out with friends three or four times a week. Not only is it expensive to eat out, but we also tend to overeat in restaurants, so our waistlines as well as our wallets are affected. (Maybe one of the small silver linings of COVID-19 is that we've developed some better habits, such as cooking and grilling out at home more often. We shall see.)

Credit cards make it all the more enticing to eat out. How many folks do you see paying a dinner bill with cash anymore? Yet if we pay with credit and do not pay off the balance each month, then we are financing our dinner. Things like meals should be pay-as-we-go, and not financed with a credit card.

Dining out is certainly a fast way to lose a lot of your monthly income and, for many people, is one of the slipperier budget items to manage. Control of this key expenditure is managed only by replacing the habit with a less expensive one, like cooking at home.

BAD HABIT #3: USING CREDIT CARDS IRRESPONSIBLY

The financial elephant in the room is, no doubt, credit cards—the root of all financial evil, the one thing that will wreck a budget in a New York minute, the one thing we must control before we can save and invest. Yet in a digital economy we need credit cards (or debit cards) to handle our transactions.

Remember the 1983 movie *Trading Places* with Eddie Murphy and Dan Aykroyd? When the police arrest Louis Winthorpe III, he brags that they don't give out all those credit cards to anyone—he can charge goods and services all over the world! Back in the '80s, you couldn't get a credit card without a job—credit cards were only for the affluent. (In my family, we carried cash.) Today, it is a digital, credit-card world for practically everyone. If you don't pay off that credit card each month, not only are you paying an exorbitant rate of interest, but you are now financing all of your basic living expenses.

Credit cards are convenient (yes!) and they often provide financial fraud protection, which is a legitimate benefit. But you must control your credit cards, or they will control you. Banks

P.O. Box 856
112 Staton Road
Greenville, NC 27835
Telephone: 252-317-3237
Fax: 252-756-2297 · Cell: 252-714-8915
E-Mail: jimwhitehurst@coastalagro.com

COASTAL
AgroBusiness, Inc.

Jim Whitehurst
President & CEO

carry a balance and they earn interest. It is
ofitable businesses in America. As Einstein is
g: "He who understands compound interest
esn't, pays it."

nd who, after college, bought clothes with
e card and paid the monthly minimum.
aid. "I can buy my clothes and pay $35 per
tting it for free!" No! If you buy a winter
id pay cash, it costs you $1,000. If you
for $1,000 and put it on a department
% and pay the monthly minimum of
ke 37 months to pay off and cost you
pay me (more) later . . .

...u forget the department stores that give you a discount
for opening a card with them. They may give a discount on the
goods up front, but unless you pay off the card immediately,
they make a huge financial return on the interest. Store credit
cards are the most profitable item in the store, and the store
becomes the invisible banker.

Rent-to-own arrangements and "no payments for twenty-
four months" at the furniture store work similarly to credit
cards and are almost never a good deal. Customers are typically
caught by not being able to pay in full by the end of the twenty-
four months. The interest is then due at maximum rates, some
nearing 30% APR, which is what the store planned all along (so
I guess it is a good deal for *them*). Next Moose and Rocco show
up at your door to repossess the furniture. Don't let a store
salesperson talk you into the "deal of the day."

I've heard some folks boast they can pay for all of their
vacations by taking advantage of their credit card's rewards
program. They run up a balance to accumulate rewards points,

then open up a new card with an introductory rate to pay down the older cards and run up more rewards points. I've even heard of people having forty different cards they keep up with on a spreadsheet. This is not a wise practice and will catch up with all but the most meticulous practitioner. Remember that there is no such thing as a free lunch. (And I seriously doubt anyone can pay for all of their vacation expenses this way.)

If you're going to use plastic, use one primary credit card (with maybe a second for backup if the first is not accepted everywhere) and pay it off in full each month, or stick with a debit card and pay for everything right away. Avoid store credit cards; for most people, they are not worth the savings in the long run. If you are going to use a rewards card, I recommend choosing cash-back cards. Taking the cash and buying your own plane tickets or other items is almost always a better decision than purchasing the "deals" offered through the card, which are usually overpriced.

A caveat: If you have gotten into financial trouble that has damaged your credit score (a high score is better than a low score), there may be an argument for having more than one credit card. Part of your credit score is derived from your credit utilization ratio—that is, how much of your available credit you are using. If you are using the maximum (even if the available amount is relatively low), that can lower your score. If you are using a small portion of what you could borrow, that can increase your score. So by having multiple cards you may be able to increase your available credit, but to get the benefit for your credit score, *you must not use that credit*. If you have a low credit score, before pursuing a multi-card strategy, do your research and maybe even talk to a credit counselor to determine what will work for you.

BAD HABIT #4: BUYING THINGS ON SALE

We all love a good deal, so if you can find something you need on sale, great. But don't get sucked into buying something *because* it is on sale. Getting 40% off is not a bargain for stuff you didn't need or want in the first place. It just means you convinced yourself you had to have it. But you still paid $60 for that $100 item that you didn't need to spend the $60 on in the first place. How many times have you found a shirt in your closet with the sale tags still on it three years later?

What if you're getting an extra 20% on top of the 40% off? Then it's a good deal, right? Wrong. First, the price is not as good as it sounds, because that extra 20% makes the price $48, not $40 (the 20% is off the $60, not the $100), so it's 52% off, not 60% off. Second, the merchant is discounting something that hasn't sold well, maybe for a reason. If you don't need (or really want) it, even at 52% off, it's still not a bargain. In addition, if you finance the purchase by signing up for the store credit card and then pay only the minimum, you could negate most of your advantage by paying an extra 25–30% in interest charges.

In a nutshell, if you're not going to use it, it's not a deal.

BAD HABIT #5: BUYING EXTENDED WARRANTIES

Let me start off by saying I love Best Buy, and I've owned their stock for years. However, I don't love that they try to sell me an extended warranty on nearly everything I buy. (I actually was pitched an extended warranty on something that cost only $60.) They have studied and understand just the right price point to get you sucked in, making warranties and gift cards the two most profitable items in the store.

I don't recommend buying any extended warranties— even if Ice-T thinks you need one on your car. If you need an extended warranty, you probably can't afford what you're buying in the first place. Buy products that you have confidence in up front, including the manufacturer's warranty. Consider independent sources such as *Consumer Reports* that give you an unbiased viewpoint. For most things, the longer the warranty, the higher the quality. If the item does break, it usually happens within the manufacturer's warranty period, when the extended warranty doesn't pay out at all. Do your homework on the front end and buy a TV set with a low defect rate; that way you can play the odds that it won't break.

You can rationalize buying an extended warranty on anything if you consider one transaction at a time. Sure, if that item breaks, you saved money. But only by rejecting all of the extended warranties in the aggregate will you save money over time. Be positive that you've made a good buy and say no to the extended warranty. Bonus: You won't have to remember whether you bought one on this or that—because you know you don't buy any of them.

BAD HABIT #6: LISTENING TO THE TRIPLE F

I enjoy the show *American Greed* narrated by Stacy Keach, but perhaps for a different reason than the producers might think. Invariably, many shows depict a Bernie Madoff–type who dupes people out of their hard-earned savings by using a Ponzi scheme, in which early investors are paid "returns" using money from newer investors. The show tends to focus solely on the crook and his fraud and how he swindled the victims out of their life savings.

Instead, I like to focus on how any person could give an almost complete stranger all of their money to invest. Yet I'll bet you many of these same folks don't trust the stock market for investing—they deem it too risky, or just don't understand it, or both. However, a slick-talking grifter can charm their socks off; they are as mesmerized by the individual as they are the investment promise, which of course is nearly impossible to achieve.

The original Ponzi was the Italian American Charles Ponzi. He was running his schemes in the 1920s, so Ponzi schemes are a century old, yet we still have crooks running them and always will. Usually the schemes are perpetuated by selling to what is known as the Triple F (FFF)—friends, family, and fools (that is, folks who are gullible).

Paul Burks's claim to fame was an investment opportunity called Zeek Rewards, where you could share in the "profits" from Zeekler, a penny auction site. (In a *penny auction*, bidders usually pay a fee to have the right to bid on items that usually go for "pennies on the dollar.") Zeek Rewards was hot in 2011, and all kinds of people—doctors, lawyers, businesspeople—were jumping in and making money. Some even mortgaged their homes to invest. The successful investors giddily showcased their quick returns on Facebook. When it all came crashing down, it was one of the biggest Ponzi schemes in US history: $900 million and about a million victims.

But are the victims really victims? *Caveat emptor.* Buyer beware. Burks himself said, "Don't blame me. I never told anyone to invest money they couldn't afford." Should we blame the regulators who were slow in getting the scheme stopped? The successful investors who got out in time couldn't care less; only the ones who lost money did—and they became the "victims." It's easy to blame the other guy when you get duped, but looking in the mirror may be more revealing. The proponents were claiming 125% returns in ninety days, which is just not believable.

I'm 100 percent sure there are more Ponzi schemes around the corner, and it is up to each of us not to fall for them. The old saying "If it sounds too good to be true, it probably is" should be changed to "If it sounds too good to be true, don't give them your money no matter what your friends tell you."

(For more on this topic, read *Don't Fall for It: A Short History of Financial Scams* by Ben Carlson.)

■■■

Do any of those bad habits look familiar?

If earlier you found your money personality was a Spendthrift, you may have a penchant for the first three habits—buying from convenience, eating out excessively, and using credit cards irresponsibly.

Shoppers may see habit #4—buying things on sale—as their primary tripping hazard.

Savers may exhibit fewer bad spending habits, but may get caught buying things on sale to save money and end up dissatisfied with the lower-cost item, and they may tend to buy extended warranties from a fear of risk.

If you are an Investor, chances are your money habits are reasonably solid, but there are probably areas in which you could make changes. If nothing else, even Investors get caught in the habit of overspending on convenience.

Gamblers are most likely to get caught in habit #6—get-rich-quick schemes—and, similar to the Spendthrift, probably have a tendency towards habits #1, 2, and 3.

Looking in the mirror can be hard. Thinking about making changes can feel overwhelming. But remember that replacing old habits with better ones makes change easier. Next up, we'll take a look at the three good habits wealthy people develop and steps you can take to develop those habits.

GOOD MONEY HABITS (PRACTICES TO BUILD)

In *The* Next *Millionaire Next Door*, Dr. Sarah Fallaw presents research that is straightforward and crystal clear: the financial habits of the wealthy are different from those of the average Joe or Jane consumer. In a word, *frugality*. Being frugal and letting your money work for you while you sleep are key to building wealth. But even if you subscribe to the "you can't take it with you, so enjoy it while you can" philosophy, if you have a family, you still have an obligation to provide some financial security for your household. And you don't have to be wealthy to begin practicing these habits. You can start regardless of your current net worth and at almost any income level (I do recognize it's much harder to get started if you are living on a very modest income).

Dr. Fallaw discusses in depth the neighborhood effect and how it influences our spending, which we covered earlier. Normally when we compare ourselves to others, it will be through the lens of the neighborhood—the size of the Joneses' house and the type of car they drive, then their vacations, second homes, and private schools for the kids. In *The* Next *Millionaire*, Dr. Fallaw shares the finding that 86 percent of luxury vehicle drivers are not "rich." They may have a high income, but they are *not* millionaires—that is, despite their high income, they don't have net worth of $1 million or more. In fact, most millionaires don't own luxury cars, and they are cautious about the houses they buy—they stick with those they can easily afford. Millionaires actually have a propensity to save and to *not* consume.

I've been called "tight" with money so many times that I wondered what was wrong with me. How could I walk through a store for over an hour and walk out with nothing? My mother told me that I was like that even as a child—I could walk right past an aisle of toys. But I get it: not everyone has that built-in trait of frugality that makes saving second nature. Here are some ideas that I hope will help build that capacity.

GOOD HABIT #1: LEARN TO AVOID DEBT

My kids and I used to love to watch personal finance guru Suze Orman hold court over her callers to decide whether to spend or not to spend. (Guess what the answer usually was.) Having a lot of fine stuff may be nice, but being debt-free is liberating, so learn to pay as you go. Listen to any of Dave Ramsey's radio shows and he, too, will invariably make this point to the caller. If you are one to always worry about money, then this advice goes double. Nothing gives you peace of mind better than eliminating debt. (Both Suze and Dave are excellent resources for learning to get control over your debt.)

Practically speaking, avoiding debt means:

- Paying off your credit card bill every month.
- Avoiding taking on other forms of consumer debt.
- Paying down the debt you do have.
- Reducing your spending so that you can do the first three items.

Remember that net worth (in other words, wealth) is calculated by assets minus liabilities (debt), so if we want to build wealth, our assets need to outweigh our debts. And any time you buy something with credit, it's costing you more than it would if you paid for it in cash. If you're going to take on debt, try to take it on things that will increase in value over time. Most of us are going to have *some* debt—probably a mortgage, maybe a student loan. The key is to not be overburdened by it.

We'll talk more about reducing debt in Chapter 6.

GOOD HABIT #2: BUILD WEALTH WITH THE RIGHT ASSETS

As I said above, to build wealth, our assets must outweigh our debts. But not all assets are created equal. So what are the "right" assets?

Recall that assets are things with long-term value. Investments are assets that have the potential and expectation of an appreciation in value over time. Not all assets are necessarily good investments. To build wealth, as much as possible we want assets that are also good investments.

Recall also that your personal financial statement (PFS) lists assets from most liquid to least liquid, with cash being the most liquid and raw land being the least liquid. For most people, at least when starting to build wealth, assets with higher liquidity should make up the largest portion of their net worth—things like savings, mutual funds, stocks, and so on. This provides some cushion against any problems that may come along. We'll talk more about these options in Chapter 7.

Real estate can contribute to a strong PFS, and the wealthiest among us are often big landowners, but real estate can be a catch-22, because it's possible to be "land rich but cash poor." Selling land usually takes some time, making its conversion to cash slow. So make sure you have access to enough liquid assets before building up real estate as a major asset.

In addition, it's important to diversify among the major asset classes as much as possible. Keeping *all* cash in savings, for instance, at 0.1% APR is a risk to your long-term wealth, as inflation will eat away at any future purchasing power. So while we want some funds in cash, we know that in order to maintain our buying power we need some investments that beat inflation. But keeping all your funds in higher-risk investments is also not a good strategy. Different parts of the market—say tech stocks, commodities, and government bonds—will perform differently based on economic conditions and other factors, so investing in multiple areas can help manage risk. We'll talk more about diversification in Chapter 7.

Your House: Good Asset or Not? A house often makes up a significant portion of a personal financial statement, so we know it's an asset. But is it a good one?

I agree with Robert Kiyosaki's comments about houses in *Rich Dad Poor Dad*. (Kiyosaki has been praised as one of the all-time financial greats yet is sometimes considered controversial in his viewpoints.) He states that while a house is an asset, it's also a liability. Think about the expenses associated with home ownership: costs of repairs, landscaping, property taxes, and so on. It can become a money pit.

Additionally, we tend to buy more house than we need (the Joneses effect); we often borrow to pay for a house without putting down much cash; and in most areas, houses don't appreciate as fast as we think they will. So while it's an asset that can increase in value over time, if you sink all your money into your home, it's difficult to handle any big emergency that may come along. In other words, there is a lot more liquidity and flexibility with a $300,000 investment fund than with a $300,000 investment in your house.

And what happens when the next recession comes along and your mortgage is under water, as happened to many folks in the 2008 recession? Negative equity (you owe more on your house than it is worth to another buyer) rears its ugly head. On top of that, you could lose your job right when a poor housing market hits, forcing you to discount the price even further to sell quickly. Your largest asset on your PFS just dropped enough to bring your net worth down to zero or worse. Sound familiar?

Bottom line: Yes, your house is an asset that gets listed on your PFS, but from a practical standpoint, you might be better off thinking of it as a necessity and a cost of living rather than as an investment. If your house and your retirement fund are the only things that make up your net worth, then it's time to rethink how your PFS looks to a financial observer. (More on mortgages in the next chapter.)

Other Assets That Are Not Really Assets. There are plenty of things you own that may be assets to you but are not what a banker would consider assets, such as furniture, jewelry, appliances, clothes, and so on. No banker will be impressed with little cash and a lot of furniture. These types of "assets" typically do not even get listed on a PFS because they depreciate so quickly that they are more often considered expenses rather than assets. And no matter how good you think you are on eBay, they will take longer to sell and net less than you think.

This is not to say you don't need these types of personal assets, but spend wisely. All of these items fall into a huge range of need versus want, meaning we must have clothes, furniture, and appliances to live (need), but we don't need an excessive amount of them (want). Remember the old riddle: What is the difference between a $5,000 Rolex and $100 Timex? Answer: The Timex keeps better time. And by all means avoid financing these types of purchases with monthly payments (credit cards or store deals), no matter how good the interest rate is supposed to be (and remember, don't buy the extended warranty).

Two other things that might be assets you list on your PFS but are not good assets and are rarely considered investments: cars and boats. A new car depreciates 20 percent the minute you drive it off the lot. And if you financed the full amount, that instant depreciation means you now owe more on the car than it is worth. A better option is to buy a two-year-old car that hasn't had a model change. Better still, buy only a car you can pay cash for. Don't fall for the salesperson's pitch: "How much can you afford per month?" What a loaded question. The salesperson is not your financial advisor—you are.

It's not difficult to understand how we fall for new cars—they are one of the most, if not the most, heavily advertised products in the world. (Plus, they smell great and—full disclosure—I've been guilty of buying new cars on occasion.) However, we use our car every day as a necessary utility. Expensive cars are for show only, not for wealth building.

Additionally, leasing a car is rarely a good idea. You have a depreciating asset that you never own free and clear. You may decide to lease anyway, because you want a new car every three years and don't want to deal with maintenance on an aging vehicle. In that case, the devil is in the details, as they say—watch out for mileage caps and wear-and-tear limits in the lease.

Likewise, a boat should never be regarded as an investment. For most of us, a boat is an expensive hobby, a liability risk, and a money pit. (More disclosure: I do own a half-share of a twenty-footer.) For most people, I'd not recommend buying a boat, especially with borrowed money. If you do buy one, pay cash; that way at least you know you can afford the size you choose. As the saying goes, a boat owner's two happiest days are the day they buy their boat and the day they sell it! Instead, I recommend you find some good friends with a boat, use theirs, and buy their gas every time—that's a much better financial plan.

We'll talk more about how to prioritize building the right assets in the next chapter and then about specific assets and investments in Part Three.

GOOD HABIT #3: USE ANNUAL AND ZERO-BASED BUDGETING

One of the most common pieces of financial advice is to develop a budget and stick to it. Yet this is often easier said than done when in our digital, convenient, credit-card world, it is so easy to spend. Let's look at budgeting possibilities . . . and we're going to think outside the box on this one.

Monthly Budget. Many people try to use a monthly budget—identifying and managing regular monthly expenses such as mortgage, utilities, and groceries. But to be honest, I'm not a big fan of monthly budgets. They seem to work well if both you and your spouse are good with money and keep up with your spending on a spreadsheet. But to me, the book title *Everything Is Obvious: Once You Know the Answer* is a good description of monthly budgeting: that is, if you know what your monthly spend is, then a monthly budget is the answer. But most people *don't* know what their monthly spend is.

The problem is that there are way too many expenses that don't fit neatly into that monthly box. For instance, insurance comes due every six or twelve months. Household repairs that are neglected become a problem or, worse, an emergency. And how many people remember to budget every month for birthdays, wedding gifts, and car repairs? Life happens. Since we don't budget these things, our monthly answer is wrong.

In addition, we see monthly payments advertised everywhere: house, car, credit cards, as well as cable TV and subscriptions. Most of the time, monthly payments are promoted to make something seem more affordable. But having to set up everything on a monthly payment may be a clue that we can't really afford something and are trying to make it affordable by squeezing it into that neat, convenient, monthly box. Anything seems justifiable when marketers can show you it costs just $39 per month. But your budget is no concern to them once they get you set up on those monthly recurring credit card charges, and ten things at $39 per month add up to $4,680 per year. Even charities advertising on TV want you pay "only $11 per month." Everything is affordable and convenient per month—until it's not. (Pro tip: When given the option to pay up front and receive a discount, it almost always makes financial sense to take the discount and eliminate monthly payments.)

Furthermore, attempting to save anything within that monthly box space can turn out to be a futile effort. Forced savings from your monthly pay can help, but trouble lurks when all those monthly charges show up on your credit card statement and you begin to carry a balance at 12% interest while your investment of your monthly savings returns only 6%. Saving becomes a futile effort, like treading water in the deep end rather than swimming over to the other side of the pool where wealth is built.

Annual Budget. The better view is to shift our paradigm from a monthly budget to an annual budget. Most of us can see the monthly "answer" more clearly if we start with our total annual spend, which usually gives us an obvious confirmation that our initial monthly budget was way too low. An annual budget gives us a truer picture of *all* of our cash flow and where it goes.

To get started on an annual budget, there are plenty of budget worksheets online. These can help remind you of the less frequent expenditures you might need to make. You can also go through your checkbook or bank statements for the past year to identify your spending patterns and specifics. Don't forget to count the cash you take out of the ATM—do you know where it goes? Some credit cards also provide a categorized breakdown of your annual spend with them.

With an annual budget, you'll quickly see if you are getting ahead or falling behind, and if credit card debt is funding your demise. You also get a far better idea of what things cost. That daily $10 lunch out at work becomes $200 per month but a whopping $2,000-plus per year. When you're *sure* you've included everything (and I mean everything, because an annual budget won't lie, but a monthly one will), you can take your total spend and divide it by twelve to get a monthly number, a *true* monthly number. I guarantee it will be higher than what you originally had down, especially if you're married (with two potential overspenders rather than just one).

Zero-Based Budget. Another way to shift the budget paradigm is to start at zero and build from the ground up, using what's called a *zero-based budget*. This method is popular with business CFOs in that it helps identify necessary spending—we must spend at least this many dollars to stay in business—and then helps prioritize what to spend rather than just fund everything requested by the various departments. Each and every expense must be justified. Not only does a zero-based budget help identify wasteful spending, but it can also help identify less useful spending that can be reallocated to higher priorities.

Going through this exercise with your personal finances can similarly expose wasteful spending (and we all have some) and prioritize discretionary spending. As those of us who are married know, even two small "departments" can cause overspending.

I suggest you start with the annual budget described above. Identify all your spending from the past year. Then, with that as a reference, start at zero and build a budget from scratch. Begin with the absolutely necessary expenses, then progress to discretionary spending, working through every single expense. This exercise will demonstrate where your discretionary spending is going, thus empowering you to make changes in your spending habits.

Using a zero-based budget will generate some discussion (healthy, I hope) about what your household needs are and what you truly value. For those who are married, I trust both spouses will value paying the mortgage or the rent, but for discretionary spending, one spouse might love eating out and getting babysitters while the other prefers clothes or cars. By creating an annual budget from the bottom (zero) up, you can force-rank what you truly value and make sure you are spending on the things that are most important to you. I also guarantee you this approach will show you where you can cut back if you stay disciplined.

Ideally, you will include a forced savings component in your zero-based budget so money is transferred to your savings before any discretionary funds get spent. With that approach, the chances of your successfully saving will be much greater than if you try to squeeze in some savings only if you happen to think about it each month.

Rather than trying to force everything into a monthly box, use an annual budget and/or a zero-based budget and you will find your budget "answer" becomes "obvious." *Seeing* where our money goes helps make sense of our financial situation. It is possible you will realize (or already know) your income is too low to be sustainable and you need to find a higher-paying job, start building the skills to do so, or seek some other form of assistance. However, for most of us, it's our spending habits, not our incomes, that are the culprits standing in the way of building wealth.

CHAPTER 6

A BLUEPRINT FOR BUILDING WEALTH

PUT YOUR OUTDOOR WORK IN ORDER
AND GET YOUR FIELDS READY; AFTER
THAT, BUILD YOUR HOUSE.
—PROVERBS 24:27 NIV

WE'VE COVERED THE FIRST two components of financial discipline: increasing financial literacy and developing good money habits. The third component is following a plan. In this chapter we'll go over the Wealth Pyramid as your blueprint for building wealth. And just as a reminder, building wealth is not about showing off or dying with the most toys—while wealth may allow you a more comfortable life, it's first and foremost about creating security for your family.

THE WEALTH PYRAMID

To develop a plan for building wealth, think of a pyramid: you need strong foundational blocks at the bottom before you can put more blocks on top. Figure 1 shows what a strong Wealth Pyramid looks like.

Figure 1: The Wealth Pyramid

You'll notice the Wealth Pyramid has three main layers of building blocks: Foundational Security, Funding the Future, and Building Wealth. We'll talk through each in detail below, but generally speaking, you should be starting at the bottom early in life—say, as you begin your adult life or professional career—and progressing up the Wealth Pyramid as you mature. By retirement, you want to be near the top of the pyramid, not worrying about foundational matters but rather feeling secure in your financial position for the foreseeable future.

While the information below is presented in a linear fashion, life is not always so neat and methodical. You may start some of the higher blocks simultaneously with lower blocks, and how quickly you progress is heavily dependent on your life situation, but overall the metaphor of building layer by layer holds.

FOUNDATIONAL SECURITY LAYER

Building a strong financial foundation begins with getting the basics in place and then setting some goals for the future. By spending some time on increasing your financial literacy and understanding the fundamentals of personal finance, you will be able to better manage your finances and avoid potential land mines. Placing an early premium on financial matters will go a long way towards building wealth over time. Let's look at some of the specifics of your financial foundation.

GETTING STARTED BLOCK

As you begin your adult life, if you plan to get married and have kids, you will increase your odds of building wealth if you establish your career first, then get married, and then have children. This is not any judgment on your personal choices; it's simply an observation that financial success comes more easily when things proceed in that order.

Developing financial restraint early on will increase your odds of long-term success. For example, you may be beginning your professional life with student debt. Develop a plan to pay it down, and resist the urge to buy the shiny new things (with more debt) to look the part of a successful young professional. Having nicer things can come later. Your business colleagues certainly understand and will appreciate the fact that you are just getting started in your career.

EMERGENCY SAVINGS BLOCK

As you begin building your Wealth Pyramid, one of the first blocks to establish is a contingency fund. This is money that you have available in cash in case of emergencies and is usually kept in a standard bank account (checking or savings or money market) so it is easily accessible.

Start with the proverbial three to six months of salary as a minimum base to cover unexpected expenses and emergencies. We'll build from there. (For inspiration read *The Richest Man in Babylon*: "I again saved each tenth copper, for now I had formed the habit and it was no longer difficult." "I . . . hid it away. And . . . I was no shorter of funds, than before. I noticed little difference . . ."

"What each of us calls our 'necessary expenses' will always grow to equal our incomes unless we protest to the contrary.")

Again, resist unnecessary expenses at this stage. If you're just starting out, fancy cars, clothes, and watches will raise a red flag to others; better to be unpretentious to build your professional integrity. If you are further along in life and playing financial catch-up, be honest with yourself about your habits to date—have they been solid? If they need improvement, now you know where to start. If they are solid, well done, and keep at it.

DEBT ELIMINATION BLOCK

Our next block involves the elimination of debt. If you have incurred credit card debt or other high-interest consumer debt, one of your top priorities is to eliminate it. Other than always having an emergency fund, it makes little sense to start investing in the stock market with expected returns of, say, 8% when you have a mountain of credit card debt at 15%. Whether you tackle the smallest balance first or the one with the highest interest rate first, what counts is that you take a disciplined and committed approach to eliminating this form of debt.

Nearly everyone who is in debt will have to address credit card balances before they can regain control of their life. I can't improve on what Dave Ramsey advises; he's great at debt reduction systems, and I would recommend him to anyone who needs a total debt reduction system with a bit of coaching along the way. NerdWallet and similar websites can also give good advice; however, I remind you that they may be getting paid by the same credit card companies that helped you get into debt in the first place. I have seen many sites that run *great* articles on how to eliminate credit card debt—right next to ads for Visa and Mastercard.

If you are early in your career and life, you may have college loans. Compared to revolving credit, student loan debt may be relatively "good" debt at a low interest rate. Some people like to get rid of all debt as quickly as possible, which is not a bad thing, but it is a reasonable practice to maintain this type of low-interest debt as you begin to build your self-funding savings—our next step.

SELF-FUNDING SAVINGS BLOCK

Once you have eliminated any high-cost debt, it's time to build enough savings that you can avoid consumer debt (e.g., credit cards) altogether and instead "self-fund" by purchasing with cash as you go. (For inspiration, see *The* Next *Millionaire Next Door.*) You could keep these funds in a bank account, or possibly in a mutual fund. The idea is that they are liquid enough to be available to you when you need or want to use them.

As part of your zero-based budgeting process (covered in Chapter 5), allocate some funds to cover larger contingencies, so you can easily handle a repair bill or medical expense that is more than your emergency savings could handle.

Additionally, analogous to an insurance policy, we want to protect ourselves against repair or replacement risk on items we purchase. For example, instead of spending $100 on an extended product warranty, reserve those funds for yourself to cover any unforeseen repair, product replacement, and so on.

Finally, if you want to buy something, use self-funding savings that are earmarked for that purpose. Don't have enough in this account? Save up enough to pay cash. If you put a purchase on your credit card, say for fraud-protection purposes or for cash-back rewards, have enough cash saved to pay it off in full *immediately*.

INSURANCE BLOCK

Think of insurance as a risk management tool. It doesn't necessarily help *build* wealth, but it *protects* wealth. Whatever policies you purchase, be sure the premiums are included in your annual budget.

Start by making sure you have adequate medical insurance at work, through private insurance, or through one of the exchanges. A single medical emergency can throw an uninsured person into a bankruptcy situation. Next, protecting your income is important. This can be accomplished by purchasing disability insurance if it is not already provided by your employer. Then comes renter's or homeowner's insurance, which is needed to replace your assets if a disaster occurs.

Depending on your situation, it may be appropriate to look at life insurance to protect your family's financial security should you or your spouse die. Insurance contracts are notoriously complex, so I lean towards buying a straightforward term life insurance policy, in which you pay a premium for coverage over a set period of time. When the term expires, the coverage expires, and if you haven't used it (which means you haven't died!), the policy is done. Term life insurance premiums are lower than those for more complex whole life insurance policies, which are often illustrated with cash value and which some people may call an "investment." By buying the term policy, you can use the difference in premiums to invest in something else (not an insurance policy). You've protected your family in the event of your death, but you can control the investment portion and possibly achieve better returns than what a whole life policy offers. It's easy to shop and compare term rates online; focus on plain vanilla insurance that insures against death with the lowest possible premiums from a reputable insurance company.

HOUSE/MORTGAGE BLOCK

The final item in the Foundational Security layer of the Wealth Pyramid is your home. Depending on where you live, it may be more feasible to rent than to buy, but if done correctly, as we discussed in the prior chapter, a house is an asset with which you can build owner's equity. Owner's equity is simply the dollar amount of the house that you own outright—that is, the principal you've paid. For example, if you bought a $300,000 house and put down $50,000 up front and have paid another $50,000 in principal (remember you've also paid interest), you have $100,000 in owner's equity (the bank has the other $200,000). And if you pay down principal faster than your mortgage requires, you not only avoid interest but also build equity faster.

If you are going to buy a home, here's how to do it smartly:

Don't buy more than you can afford. Your mortgage banker wants to qualify you for the maximum size house possible, but just because some loan company says you can afford it doesn't mean you can. And it's possible to have a great credit score while still being up to your eyeballs in debt. Do not succumb to Rocket Mortgage, LendingTree, or similar websites' advice on how much house you can afford. They are not your fiduciary—you are. There is good news, however. When rates are low, you can "afford" more house. (Even though interest rates are climbing as I write this, looking back as far as the 1970s, rates in the early 2020s are still historically low.) The interest may be tax deductible as well, though due to changes to the standard deduction in 2018, for many people this is less likely than it once was.

Get a 15-year mortgage and put 20% down. When purchasing a house, take out a 15-year mortgage and put down 20% up front. So if you're buying that $300,000 house, you need to save $60,000 for the down payment. (Start early!) My understanding is that the 15-year/20% approach is the norm in Canada, but in the US, many people take out 30-year mortgages. (I've even seen fifty-year-olds take out a 30-year refinanced mortgage to get a lower interest rate. Do you really want to make house payments until you're eighty?) It becomes much harder to build owner's equity with a 30-year mortgage.

The difference between a 15-year loan amortization and a 30-year is not difficult to illustrate, and can be found anywhere online (search for "mortgage amortization calculator"); however, be warned that the mortgage companies would rather have you *not* understand it. In a nutshell, you pay *way* more interest on a 30-year mortgage than on a 15-year.

Our example in Chapter 4 used a $300,000, 5% fixed-rate mortgage to compare a 30-year amortization with a 15-year amortization. After ten years of monthly payments, the person with the 30-year mortgage has about $56,600 in equity; the person with the 15-year mortgage has $176,100—over three times as much. By the time the house is fully paid off, the person with the 30-year mortgage has spent $580,000 and the person with the 15-year has spent only $427,000—over $150,000 less.

Pro tip: Instead of giving your kids money for a big wedding, give them the same amount for a down payment on a house. Give them the best financial start possible.

Avoid adjustable rates and balloons. Stay away from adjustable-rate mortgages (ARMs) and balloon loans. An adjustable rate means that the interest rate you pay changes periodically (typically annually); these products often have a low teaser rate to hook you in, but when rates go up, you can be in for a big shock.

Similarly, a balloon loan means you pay a low amount (sometimes interest only) for a period of time and then pay the loan in full at a certain point. When the principal comes due, most people don't actually pay it; instead, they refinance the loan or sell the property. However, if your financial situation changes, or if the economy as a whole changes (for example, if the stock market declines as it did in 2008), you may not be in a position to refinance at a favorable rate and real estate sales may be slow or housing prices lower than you anticipated.

Adjustable rates and balloons will do a great job of keeping you in debt. Keep your mortgage as simple as possible. Stick with an easier-to-understand 15-year mortgage, where you can build equity much faster and more predictably. Understand that while your house is not a great investment, it is likely one of your biggest assets, so it's better to have a plan to pay for it rather than to finance it in perpetuity.

Avoid reverse mortgages. Finally, don't do a reverse mortgage, no matter what Magnum, P.I., says. (Is he (a) a TV-show character or (b) an expert on reverse mortgages?) Reverse mortgages are exactly that, the reverse of a mortgage: instead of paying off your loan and building equity, you are taking money and decreasing your home equity. So in essence you are going into debt by taking a loan against your home, and since these products are available only to those over 62, you are doing this at the point you are likely to be entering retirement, just at the time when we all should strive to be debt-free. Don't trust any television ad when it comes to financial matters, housing or otherwise.

FUNDING THE FUTURE LAYER

Foundational work may feel like just that—work. And a lot of work. Give yourself a pat on the back if you've got a solid foundation built. In the Funding the Future layer, it's time to start thinking longer term.

RETIREMENT FUNDS BLOCK

Retirement savings are your next priority. You can't rely only on Social Security—it was never intended to fund all your living expenses in retirement. Plus, who knows if it will be there when you retire, so it's up to you to plan ahead for regular living expenses (including inflation), healthcare (the cost is always increasing), and increased travel or whatever other plans you have for your newly freed-up time. In my opinion, the top retirement funding priorities are employer-sponsored plans and Roth IRAs.

Employer-sponsored plans. There are two main types of employer-sponsored retirement plans: defined benefit and defined contribution.

With a *defined benefit plan* your employer agrees to provide a clearly delineated benefit in your retirement. For example, you get a monthly payment of a set dollar amount as long as you live, or you get a lump sum at retirement. These are also called *pension plans*. If you do have a pension, be sure you know how it works. Many plans have vesting at various anniversaries (for example, the amount you receive in retirement may jump up for every ten years of service), so don't lose money by leaving your employer shortly before you would vest at a higher dollar amount. However, pension plans are becoming less and less common due to the financial liabilities that companies end up carrying. You are more likely to have a defined contribution plan.

In a *defined contribution plan*, such as a 401(k) or 403(b), employees make pre-tax contributions from their paycheck into a retirement account. Since these are pre-tax funds going into the account, they are taxed when you take them out of the account in retirement. (Note: Defined contribution plans have a maximum amount you can contribute each year, and if you are age fifty or over, you can also make extra "catch-up" contributions. The amounts you are allowed to contribute change periodically, so always check the current year's limits.)

Employers often match a portion of employees' contributions, up to a maximum amount. If you do get an employer match, be sure to contribute enough to your 401(k) or 403(b) to take full advantage of it. You should probably do this even if you are, for example, paying off student loan debt (in the Foundational Security layer of the pyramid). If you don't, you are leaving free money on the table.

Defined contribution plans have investment options—typically a variety of mutual funds—that employees can put their money in, the idea being that their retirement accounts grow over time. Even if you haven't invested in the stock market anywhere else, you are likely to be invested in it via your retirement plan.

One thing to realize about defined contribution plans: the risk that employers used to take guaranteeing pension payments (which meant they needed to invest their money wisely to have enough to make those payments) now falls on you, the employee. It's your job to make decisions about the funds you contribute to your retirement plan—and it's entirely possible to lose money, so you need to pay attention to how much you contribute, how you allocate those funds, and the performance of the account over time.

There are many kinds of employment-related retirement plans out there, and even sole proprietors can have employer-based plans. Do your research and talk to a financial professional for help on determining the right approach for your situation.

Roth IRA. An *IRA* is an individual retirement account. A *traditional IRA* is typically funded with pre-tax dollars, so you don't pay taxes on the funds until you start withdrawing money in retirement. A *Roth IRA* is funded with after-tax funds, so you can take it out tax-free in retirement, which is especially beneficial if your tax rate is higher then. For most people, a Roth IRA provides tax advantages for the long term, so chances are you'll want to contribute the maximum. IRAs, too, are often funded with mutual funds, but can also be funded with stocks, bonds, and other investment vehicles. Note: As with 401(k)s and other retirement plans, IRAs have limits on the amount you can contribute each year and are subject to income limitations; always be sure to check the current limits, and talk to your CPA or financial advisor if you have questions about your situation.

COLLEGE SAVINGS BLOCK

The next priority in Funding the Future is college savings for your kids (if applicable). You'll notice I put retirement savings as a higher priority than college savings. That's because you need to make sure your retirement and long-term care needs are taken care of first. If you fund your children's education without saving enough for yourself, you run the risk of a domino effect wherein the younger generation's future savings go to support the older generation, and the cycle continues. So fund your own future first; *then* shift to building wealth for future generations. This means your kids may need to work for their education (or at least part of it). Furthermore, you may *want* them to have to fund at least part of their own education to help develop their own good financial habits.

However, many of us do help fund our children's education. If you plan to do so, keep that money in a separate account dedicated to that purpose. One option is a 529 plan. While 529 plans come with some tax benefits, they also come with regulations and restrictions. I prefer investing in the stock market for education funding. I'd rather spend time reading *The Value Line Investment Survey* than learning the whys and wherefores of the government-controlled 529. Also, managing your own education investments can be a great opportunity for you and your kids to learn about the stock market and various investing strategies. They can be a lot more straightforward than you might think. (More in Part Three.)

Don't forget there are many other sources for college funding: scholarships, grants, student loans, military options, work-study programs. Similar to a mortgage, student loans, if taken at a low rate and handled properly, may be "good" debt, but do your due diligence and help your student choose smartly.

One of my colleagues tells the story of his parents putting his college savings into a trust. In middle school, he was told that he could use the money however he wanted when he reached eighteen, but that he wouldn't be given any more money for college. Clever kid that he was, he considered closely where he wanted to go to school and the value of the degree versus the cost of the education. He ended up choosing a strong public school over a number of more expensive private schools, worked extraordinarily hard in high school to get a scholarship, and then got to keep the money in the trust fund. I hope you teach your kids to think so strategically about their finances and life choices.

BUILDING WEALTH LAYER

By the time we reach the top layer of the pyramid, ideally we've laid all the blocks in the Foundational Security and Funding the Future layers without any debt except a 15-year mortgage. We are building home equity, we are self-funding all of our contingencies, we have fully funded our retirement needs, and we sleep well at night when it comes to money issues. I know this might sound like a lot—and it is no small feat. But with patience and consistency, you can build up these funds for your family's security. And then the fun begins . . .

The Building Wealth layer entails a greater focus on the investing world. As noted earlier, you likely already have stock market investments in your retirement plan (and possibly for education or other funding blocks), so chances are you are already investing in some form. But now you can look to broader purposes. Think of this layer first as a supplement to the Funding the Future layer; then, as you move to the peak, you can focus on wealth-building for legacy, philanthropic, and other similar purposes. Part Three will get into investing in more detail, so here I just want to give you a feel for how to prioritize the building of your investments.

DIVERSIFIED MARKET FUND BLOCK

At this point we want to focus on basic stock market investing and avoid risky "alternative" investments or any all-in investment opportunity (a.k.a. scheme), so first, I suggest dipping your toe into investment waters with a diversified market fund.

A diversified stock market index fund basically lets you buy a "basket" of the entire market. You will get the ups and downs of the full market, and since it is a diverse basket, you can stay continuously invested without having to worry about the risk of individual sectors or specific companies.

INDIVIDUAL STOCKS BLOCK

Once you're invested in the market through a market index fund (and probably through your retirement funds), move up to investing in individual stocks with a self-directed brokerage account or a broker-advised account. We discuss stock investing in greater detail in Chapter 8.

If you can start at an early age and let compound interest do its magic, then your stock portfolio can serve as additional retirement funds, savings, and investments for long-term wealth building, all in one.

OTHER INVESTMENTS BLOCK

As your wealth builds and you have more funds available to you for investing purposes, you may want to expand into real estate and other types of investments. Some of these may carry more risk, so it's smart to make sure you are financially secure should you lose money on them. More on these possibilities in Chapter 7.

WHERE ARE YOU IN BUILDING YOUR WEALTH PYRAMID?

The net worth you have right now is influenced by where you started, your job earnings and other sources of income, your family situation (such as whether you have kids and/or a stay-at-home parent in the family), and all the factors we discussed in Chapter 2 as well as your financial literacy, your money habits, and whether you've been using a plan. Generally speaking though, people in their twenties and thirties are likely to be laying Foundational Security blocks, people in their thirties and forties are probably in the Funding the Future layer, and those age forty and up may be up to the Building Wealth layer.

And to reiterate: while the Wealth Pyramid is presented linearly, of course many things could be occurring simultaneously or in a somewhat different order: you can begin building retirement savings before you buy a house, and you can fund an IRA before you consider life insurance. And we already mentioned that stocks can be used to fund college, retirement, and other blocks, especially if you have the opportunity to start early.

When you start young and build a solid foundation, time offers you a huge advantage, but you are where you are, so progress from there. We can almost all improve our financial literacy and money habits so that we can move up the pyramid. If you're feeling a bit discouraged, consider this: If you're fifty, you probably have another fifteen years of work before retirement. In that span of time, you can double your assets *twice*.

The journey to the top of the Wealth Pyramid is slow and takes discipline. Unless you were born into a wealthy family, you'll probably have to make some sacrifices to reach the peak, but attaining that level gives you the ultimate control and freedom. Knowing that any bank would jump at having you as a client is satisfying, but climbing the pyramid is not about owning a private island one day.

It is about not sweating over your monthly budget; it is freedom from needing a budget, period. As Arkad in *The Richest Man in Babylon* said, you "rebel against the slavery of a budget." It is about controlling your own finances without anyone else having a say, and having enough self-confidence not to be talked into anything. You can be debt-free if you want to be debt-free, which is a liberating experience. You don't pay a premium (through interest, fees, or penalties) when you buy things; you get discounts for paying with cash up front. Rather than being a poor consumer, you become "the bank." Climbing the Wealth Pyramid is simply about the satisfaction of achieving security for yourself and your family and your legacy.

PART THREE

THE BASICS OF INVESTING

In this last part of the book, we take the leap into investing, first starting with some definitions and then discussing basic investment strategy. While this is by no means a complete guide to investing, my hope is that it demonstrates investing is less risky than you might think and encourages you to get started.

CHAPTER 7

INVESTMENTS,
GOOD TO GREAT

THE STOCK MARKET IS FILLED WITH INDIVIDUALS
WHO KNOW THE PRICE OF EVERYTHING,
BUT THE VALUE OF NOTHING.
—PHILLIP FISHER

GROWING UP IN A family of investors, I can remember discussing our Eli Lilly stock performance and receiving nice quarterly dividend checks. Most every Sunday we would visit my grandmother and she would ask about how my stock was doing and whether it had split yet, and she'd talk about her stocks, such as Walgreens, Ryder, VF Corporation, and Wachovia.

When it comes to investments, beauty is in the eye of the beholder. Different investors have different preferences. But some investments can be better than others, and some are higher risk than others. In this chapter, we'll talk about types of financial investments. But first, a reminder . . .

WHAT IS AN INVESTMENT?

We've talked about what an investment is a couple of times now: it's an asset that is expected to appreciate (increase in value over time) and/or to produce income. Cars and boats might be assets but don't qualify as investments; furniture, clothing, and jewelry, even less so. Big houses, fancy cars, and lots of "stuff" can make you look rich, but they won't make you wealthy or deliver the real financial security needed for you and your family.

Investments, by my definition, include marketable securities like common stocks, bonds, mutual funds, exchange-traded funds (ETFs), and so on, as well as income-producing real estate. While savings accounts, certificates of deposit (CDs), and retirement plans are technically investments, savings accounts and CDs do not yield enough in a low-interest-rate environment to qualify as investments to me, and I consider retirement plans to be more of a nest egg for future living expenses rather than true investments.

Long-term stock market investing is one of the most practical ways to build wealth, but you must understand and get comfortable with the risk involved. My personal experience is that stock market investing can be volatile at times, but not risky. What's risky is running out of money as a senior. In the next section I'll try to demonstrate why—in the long term—the stock market is not as risky as you might think. The key is to have a patient perspective with a disciplined approach. In this way you can build wealth and beat inflation by taking advantage of compound interest over time.

We'll get back to stock investing, but first let's take a trip around the investment world to get a feel for the landscape and view some options.

RISK VS. REWARD

When evaluating any investment opportunity, the key consideration is the risk vs. reward tradeoff. When we say *risk*, we mean the likelihood an asset shows below-expected performance or permanently loses value. When we say *reward*, we mean the increase in value or the return on investment (ROI) we've talked about multiple times already.

In an ideal world, we'd have low risk and high reward, but that's just not the way the world works (and if someone tries to sell you that, look out for a scheme). In the real world, if you take no risk or very low risk, you tend to get a correspondingly low reward. If you take a greater amount of risk, there is often the *potential* for greater reward, though no guarantee of it. But that risk/reward analysis is what you are always taking into account, whether you realize it or not and whether your estimation of each is reasonable or not.

Taking too much risk is not advisable since your savings can be put at risk of full loss. Conversely, having everything in a low-interest savings account will guarantee that your assets will not keep up with inflation and your future purchasing power will erode over time. A portfolio of different assets is necessary to balance out these two extremes of risk. Additionally, different asset classes carry different sorts of risk. For example, bonds are sensitive to interest rate changes while stock returns are based more on company sales and profit performance. Again, a diverse portfolio helps us balance the various types of risk.

People often confuse risk with volatility. They are related terms but not synonymous. We described risk as the potential for permanent loss or underperformance. *Volatility*, on the other hand, generally refers to how much an asset's value (such as a stock price) swings up and down around its recent average price. A stock can be volatile—its price can move up and down—while still being a reasonable risk. All stocks fluctuate in value, especially in the short term, but the good ones still appreciate over time. Likewise, a stock can have little volatility but not be a good investment because it is depreciating or not keeping up with its peer (industry) group.

I suppose America has always had a bit of a maverick mentality when it comes to taking risks. The 1849 Gold Rush is a great example of our nation's get-rich-quick mindset. The lure and excitement of fast money has spurred the development of Las Vegas, state lotteries, and many other schemes. If there is a shortcut to wealth, we Americans are all-in. True investing can easily take a back seat to more exciting avenues to make money with less effort. Emotions drive behavior, and the lure and excitement of being a lottery winner (Look, honey! It just hit ten figures!) is simply too powerful an elixir to overcome boring, patient, long-term investing. When the online betting platform DraftKings became all the rage, sports betting took on a life of its own. The resolve to take a long view will be challenging, but ultimately more rewarding if done the correct way.

TYPES OF INVESTMENTS FROM LOW RISK TO HIGH RISK

Let's look at types of investments from lower risk to higher risk. As you will see, the lower the risk, the lower the potential reward (typically), and the higher the risk, the higher the potential reward. But the higher the risk, the greater chance of loss as well. I'll repeat what I said before: there is a place for both lower-risk and higher-risk investments in all portfolios.

BANK ACCOUNTS

Every one of us needs to have some money on hand for paying bills, buying groceries, handling contingencies, and so on. A bank account—checking, savings, or money market—is the most common way to store that money. Many people see the safety of keeping their earnings in a bank as a way to have their money secure and to eliminate risk of loss. It is. Peace of mind is in not losing the first dollar. Banks spend a great deal of capital on huge buildings to market to you that your money is safe and secure with them. Additionally, most banks are FDIC insured. That means the Federal Deposit Insurance Corporation, a government agency, protects up to $250,000 per depositor, per bank, per account.

So, yes, banks are safe in that sense. The downside is that bank accounts pay minimal interest. Checking accounts sometimes pay no interest at all. During the 2010s, savings accounts paid an average of less than 0.2% (some as low as 0.01%). But even with somewhat higher or upward-trending rates, say 1% or 2%, if inflation is 3% or 4%, your real rate of return stays negative and you lose buying power over time. This is not an issue if you keep only enough money in accounts for monthly expenses. But if you build up your deposits, it's a problem, because you are losing the potential of compound interest. (Banks love you for having a lot of cash on deposit with them, because those cheap deposits can be loaned out to others much more profitably.)

Bank accounts play an important role in personal finance. They offer the flexibility and liquidity needed to run our daily lives. But they should be only the basic foundation for our wealth-building goals. They should serve as our reserves in case of major repairs or expenses that may arise. However, we must step up from savings to higher-yielding investments that can give us a positive real rate of return.

CERTIFICATES OF DEPOSIT (CDS)

After bank accounts, the next safest investments are certificates of deposit, or CDs. When you purchase a CD, you agree to leave a sum of money in an account for a set period—six months, one year, five years—and at the end of that time, you get the principal back as well as interest at an agreed-upon rate. As I write, a five-year CD is earning about 1.5%, though as with savings accounts, rates are climbing. A CD might perform slightly better than a savings account and, again, it is safe in that you won't lose your money, but it's still no way to build wealth or even to beat inflation. Using our handy Rule of 72, at 1.5%, it would take 48 years to double your money. The only reason to consider buying a CD with that low a rate is if you think that interest rates will be headed negative (which occasionally has happened in some areas of the world).

So, the irony with both bank accounts and CDs is that we believe our money is safe (and if your money personality is a Saver, you are probably comfortable in this space). Yet when we look at it through the lens of financial security, we are likely losing buying power. If we are serious about our responsibility in securing our family's future, then we must move beyond bank accounts and certificates of deposit. Saving part of our income is a great first step; taking on some additional risk is necessary, however, to reach our long-term wealth goals.

TREASURY SECURITIES

The next step up from CDs is *Treasury securities* ("Treasuries"), which represent debt for the government. When you buy a Treasury, you are essentially giving the US government a loan in return for interest payments made twice a year. Treasury securities are named by the length of time to maturity. Treasury bills ("T-bills") are up to one year; Treasury notes ("T-notes") are two years to ten years; and Treasury bonds ("T-bonds") are twenty or thirty years. Many of us own Treasuries, at least indirectly, through a diversified bond mutual fund in our retirement account. Professional bond fund managers help ensure that the risk is managed properly within the fund.

Because Treasury securities are backed by the US government, they are considered extremely safe. However, if a 10-year T-note yields you only about 3%, that means it will take about 24 years to double your money. (And T-note yields dipped as low as 1% not long ago.) So not very risky but not very "safe" either. And recall that when interest rates rise, Treasury securities will go down in value since the newer issues will be more valuable at the current higher rates.

Plus, with the nation's debt at over $31,000,000,000,000 (that's trillion with a T) and counting, I believe the US government will want to keep the interest rate on that debt as low as possible. (I have changed this debt figure multiple times while writing this book—each time up!) Even at only 1%, that's still

$300 billion a year just to service our debt! And the risk of US government debt obligations will likely increase in the future. Today the US dollar is still by far the world's leading currency, but that may change. Some commentators are already suggesting that China may be a real threat; China has much motivation to see a cryptocurrency (such as its version of Bitcoin) become the world currency standard. Other countries, such as El Salvador, have adopted Bitcoin as their currency as a way to challenge the US greenback.[25] Additionally, I believe our ongoing printing of new money will weaken our currency, weaken our standing in the world order, and thus weaken our world security. Money does matter—quite a bit.

CORPORATE AND MUNICIPAL BONDS

Corporate bonds and *municipal bonds* are debt securities offered by, as you might guess, companies and municipalities. They function much the same way as Treasuries, with a variety of possible maturity periods, but with somewhat higher risk than Federal securities.

As we defined earlier, a bond represents debt for the entity issuing it. When you buy a bond, you are essentially giving the entity a long-term loan in return for interest payments, known as coupon payments. When bonds mature, the principal becomes due (that is, you get paid back the principal you loaned out). Remember that bond prices have an inverse relationship with interest rates: an increase in interest rates will reduce the value of the bond, and a decrease will increase the value of the bond.

Bonds certainly have a place in investing, and they always will. (Full disclosure: I've never bought a bond with my self-directed

INVESTMENTS, GOOD TO GREAT

accounts. Bonds to me are *way* more boring than stocks.) While bonds may be a relatively safe bet in terms of the risk of loss, that also means our returns are too low to ever meet our financial wealth goals, especially when interest rates are low. Plus, being able to predict which way interest rates are headed is a pro's job. Back in the 1980s, when Michael Lewis wrote *Liar's Poker*, the book that made him famous, the action with the Wall Streeters was in bonds, not equities (stocks). In a low-interest-rate environment, bonds are not very attractive.

REAL ESTATE

The opportunity to invest in real estate is widespread. If you own your home, you are dabbling in real estate at a basic level. Income-producing properties, such as commercial buildings or rental houses, can be great long-term investments as well. You purchase the property up front and then rent or lease it at a rate high enough to cover any mortgage payments and other property-related expenses, such as property tax and maintenance. If the income stream is attractive enough, you can build a nice financial cushion over time. Additionally, your investment property may appreciate in value.

Another option is buying land that you plan to hold and then sell when it appreciates. Or you might purchase a house, for example, to refurbish and resell quickly at a higher price, which is called *flipping*.

Beware, however, that what got us all into trouble during the Great Recession in 2008 was short-term greed in real estate. (If your money personality is Gambler, pay attention!) Being able to flip properties and make a quick profit was too enticing for many. When weighing real estate investments, take into consideration the possibility of another recession and how much risk you want to take. On top of the market risk, there are also interest rate, inflation, and vacancy factors to consider. (At this writing, inflation is a critical consideration.) And real estate is not very liquid—it takes time to sell it and turn it into cash.

Real estate investments can be wonderful, but the watch-out is to keep some liquid investments for when that inevitable next recession hits.

STOCKS AND ITERATIONS THEREOF

As we learned earlier, stocks represent equity in a company; when you buy a stock, you become an owner of the company. "The stock market" usually refers to common stocks sold on a public exchange such as the NYSE or the NASDAQ.

Stocks (as well as bonds) are known as "marketable securities" on your personal financial statement (PFS). Stocks have the advantage over real estate in that the expected returns are often comparable, yet stocks have much more flexibility due to their greater liquidity. You can sell some stock at any time and have your money in about three days. I can almost guarantee you that it will take more than three days to get your money when you decide to sell real estate, especially raw land.

Common stocks of public companies typically provide two ways for you to make a return on your investment: dividends and appreciation.

Some companies pay dividends, typically on a quarterly basis. Stockholders can take the dividends as cash or can reinvest them in the company's stock (that is, buy more shares). Since 2000, the average yield of stocks in the Standard & Poor's 500 (S&P 500) has ranged from 1.2% to 3.2%, averaging about 1.8% through 2020. That means an average stock portfolio of $10,000 would yield you $180 each year. This 1.8% yield is likely better than having your hard-earned savings sitting in a savings account, but still may not keep up with inflation.

However, your stock can also appreciate over time. If your $10,000 in stock increases in value to $11,000 by the end of the first year, then you have an annual gain of 10%. This $1,000 is your *capital gain* (increase in the value of the capital).

Your total return—dividends plus appreciation—is 11.8% for the year.

At tax time, you owe taxes on the 1.8% dividend income, but if you have not sold your stock, you don't owe any taxes on the 10% gain, because it is considered an *unrealized gain*. Only when you sell the stock, thus generating a *realized gain*, do you have to pay *capital gains tax* on it. Additionally, the length of time you hold a stock changes the tax rate paid. If you hold it for less than a year, you pay *short-term capital gains tax*; if you hold it for at least a year, it qualifies for *long-term capital gains tax*, which is a lower rate than the short-term tax rate. (Full disclaimer: These are general descriptions. I am not a CPA or tax advisor, and tax treatment of stocks can be complex. Be sure to talk to your trusted advisor about ways to manage your stock sales and tax bills wisely.)

There are ways to invest in real estate that could rival the returns enjoyed from equities, but as mentioned earlier, due to its greater liquidity, I am biased in favor of using the stock market to help meet your financial goals. Yes, the greed on Wall Street can turn all of us off from time to time, but if we look at owning stock as an investment in the future of America, then the perspective of owning small pieces of Corporate America becomes more palatable.

In addition to individual stocks, there are iterations, such as mutual funds and ETFs, that bundle stocks together so that you own a collection of stock rather than individual stocks. This is one way to reduce risk. We'll talk about these variations more in the next chapter as part of considering an investment strategy.

If you're a Saver or a Shopper, it's time to start looking at equities. As a Saver, you've shown you can tuck money away; now it's time to make a greater return on it. As a Shopper, it's time to put your savvy shopping smarts to work in a more effective manner.

ALTERNATIVE INVESTMENTS

What about alternative investments such as cryptocurrencies, annuities, gold and silver, and options and futures? These investments have a huge range of risk and reward, so I'm lumping them all together at the end here, but you know what most of them have in common? Big-ass fees to you (the consumer) and big fat commissions for the salesperson.

Bitcoin and other *cryptocurrency* products—virtual currencies that are designed to be difficult to counterfeit—are the latest (but probably not the last) investment fad. Maybe I'm wrong and cryptocurrency is not a fad, but it may take considerable time to become a proven technology. As of this writing, it is new to the scene; no one can tell you what it is or who invented it; it is way too volatile; it enables cybercrime; "mining" it consumes a lot of energy; the government will eventually regulate it; and if you invest in it, you will be competing against professional day traders. If you can master all of the above, then I think you have a future on Wall Street working at a hedge fund.

Even if you could alleviate all my doubts, that still does not make cryptocurrency a good investment—a speculation perhaps, but not an investment. At least with something like gold you own a gold bar; with Bitcoin I'm not sure what you own other than a brokerage account that says you've got $60,000 worth of "coins" in April and $30,000 worth of coins in July, which is what happened in 2021. You may be thinking, "I could lose half my money on a stock, too." Sure, if you choose the wrong ones—but when you do your research (remember to triangulate), you reduce that risk. The key lesson with cryptocurrency, as with any investment, is to do your homework, but I'd suggest you leave Bitcoin to the Gamblers.

I will make a similar argument against annuities. In an annuity, you typically pay a lump sum up front for guaranteed payments over a period of time. While a steady stream of payments might sound nice, you're locked in for the long term, which reduces your flexibility, and if the annuity doesn't keep up with future inflation, you're stuck.

Plus, annuities are complex instruments: variable vs. fixed, guaranteed period certain, single vs. joint lifetime income, principal protection (full evidence that you're getting had), B share, Bonus, L share, C share . . . the list keeps going. Most people would be wiser to spend their time learning the stock market rather than all the lingo of an annuity contract.

The one thing you can count on is that annuities are great for the sales rep and company selling them. Claiming that an annuity is "right for you" is subjective at best. There are almost always better options out there for the taking. "The devil is in the details" applies especially with annuities, since there are just too many ways to be had.

When you buy gold and other *commodities*, goods that are fungible (that is, basically the same coming from any producer), you are likely trying to maintain value against inflation. However, while gold may seem like a great investment as a precious metal and a store of value, the price is always going to be volatile. Whether the price is $1,800 an ounce or $2,800 an ounce, you still possess a gold bar that will always be a gold bar. With equities you can accomplish the same objective (beating inflation) without paying high fees to store your gold and with the stock or mutual fund being available as cash anytime. And you can't grow a gold bar the way a publicly traded company can grow its assets.

If you are convinced gold is a good investment, you can always look for a mutual fund that invests in precious metals. That way you benefit from the performance of the gold and other metals within the fund as well as from professional management that knows more about it than you do, but you keep your flexibility and liquidity as well.

Options and futures are as complicated as annuities and as inflexible as gold. An *option* gives you the right to buy something at a specific price anytime during the life of the contract. This could come in handy if, for example, you own an option to buy lumber at $1 per board and the price has gone up to $3 per board due to supply chain issues (say, during a pandemic). Luckily, if lumber is only $0.50 per board, the option does not obligate you to buy it at $1 per board (thus the term "option").

A *futures contract* is an agreement to buy or sell something on a specific date at a specific price. If you listen to the radio in agricultural states, you'll often hear "the futures report" because futures are often used with commodities like corn and soybeans. A farmer might agree to sell corn at $5 per bushel next year. Even if the price is up to $9 per bushel next year, the farmer still has to sell at $5. On the flip side, if you're the company making corn oil out of that corn, you just paid $5 per bushel instead of the going rate of $9, effectively saving $4.

These examples are gross oversimplifications of options and futures, but the idea is that both are forms of hedging your investments (that is, taking counteractions in case the market goes a different way than you expect). They *can* be forms of making money, but in that regard, they are speculation rather than investments. In a nutshell, unless you are a fortuneteller, the options deck is so stacked against you that Vegas is a better bet. (Plus, it's much easier to learn the rules of craps than it is the rules of options, no matter what the Najarian brothers say.) Leave the futures and options game to the professionals (and the Gamblers).

■■■

If all these choices seem overwhelming, go back to Chapter 6 to make sure you have built the right foundation in your Wealth Pyramid. And when you are ready to start investing for wealth-building purposes, the next chapter covers how to get started. The number one rule of investing is you have to be willing to take on some risk to increase your return. By increasing your financial literacy and educating yourself on the tradeoffs between risk and reward, you can then make better choices for long-term wealth creation.

INVESTMENTS SUMMARY: BEST TO WORST

COMMON STOCKS
Flexible, liquid, long-term performance.

REAL ESTATE
Income-producing; potential inflation hedge.

CORPORATE BONDS
Higher return than government bonds; safe.

GOVERNMENT BONDS
Safe and liquid, but returns are currently poor.

CASH BANK ACCOUNTS
FDIC-insured, safe against loss of principal,
but do not keep up with inflation.

COLLECTIBLES
(E.G., CARS, JEWELRY, ANTIQUES, ART)
May or may not appreciate; illiquid.

LIFE INSURANCE AND ANNUITIES
Good for financial protection but
not as investments; heavy commissions.

COMMODITIES
Speculative. (May as well go to Vegas—
you'll have better odds!)

CRYPTOCURRENCY (E.G., BITCOIN)
More speculative than commodities, at least as of this
writing. (Go to Vegas and put it on red or black!)

CHAPTER 8

STOCK MARKET INVESTING

THE REAL KEY TO MAKING MONEY IN STOCKS
IS NOT TO GET SCARED OUT OF THEM.
—PETER LYNCH

BACK WHEN I WAS A CHILD and our family had Eli Lilly stock (and even into my early adulthood), paper stock certificates were held in an at-home safe or perhaps in a safe deposit box at the bank. And you had to read the newspaper to find a stock's share price and trading range from the previous day, the 52-week high/low, the dividend yield, and so on.

As you can imagine, things have changed. Today people rarely hold tangible stock certificates, and the old rote, manual method of learning about and following stocks has shifted to being largely online. In fact, with computer technology, algorithms, and commission-free online trading (not to mention social media egging us on to day-trade), it may be hard to resist the frantic pursuit of quick returns. But, to be cliché, investing is a marathon, not a sprint. If we slow down, patience will win out in the long run.

Let's break down today's investment process into high-level steps and then we'll dig into each step in more detail in the upcoming sections:

1. Start **learning about the market** generally. Do a lot of reading.
2. Consider if you will go the **self-directed** or **advisor-managed** route for your investments (and you can do both).
3. Consider different **investing approaches**, choosing the strategies and styles that suit you.
4. Consider the **type(s) of equity investment(s)** you want to invest in (mutual funds, ETFs, or individual stocks).
5. Do your research to **choose individual stocks.**

Now, these steps are shown as sequential, but some can proceed simultaneously and, of course, your choices can change over time.

LEARNING ABOUT THE MARKET

We've begun enhancing our basic financial literacy in this book, but there's more to learn when you're ready to invest. Like most other areas of study, the investment sphere has its own jargon, concepts, and strategies, so your first task is to educate yourself. By taking a disciplined approach to acquiring information and knowledge, over time you will increase your understanding and at least be able to follow a conversation with others who are more experienced. Your learning curve can pick up speed more quickly than you might realize.

In the appendix I've listed my favorite books and resources that can help you with the journey. And in the section about choosing stocks, I mention a few other resources. Luckily, today you can find a lot of information online, an easier process than the one my younger self and Ronald Read navigated as we bought newspapers or headed to the library to do research.

If you need a good starting place, I suggest you begin by studying value investing, an approach in which you focus on purchasing undervalued stocks, to gain practical financial knowledge. (Value investing is the style preferred by Warren Buffett, who knows a thing or two about investing.) We'll look at that more in a moment.

SELF-DIRECTED VS. ADVISOR-MANAGED INVESTMENTS

Second, consider if you want to manage your investments yourself, which is known as *self-directed investing*, or if you want to hire a professional to do it for you, known as *advisor-managed investing*. I recommend that you invest at least a portion of your discretionary income yourself, because once you gain a comfortable intellectual understanding of the basics, your learning should be put into practice. The hands-on experience of doing your own research and making your own decisions will boost your knowledge and your confidence. Plus, when investing in individual common stocks, it is much more interesting to follow a company that you have studied and understand—you get to watch their business strategy in action.

Even if you do choose to use a professional advisor, by researching and managing at least a few of your own investments, you'll be able to ask better questions of your advisor and to understand and follow their recommendations. But remember that you, and only you, are the ultimate fiduciary for your investment decisions. Whether most of your investments are self-directed or professionally managed, the real key is that you are invested in the best possible way for yourself and your family.

INVESTING APPROACHES

Before you start picking stocks or choosing funds, it helps to have an understanding of different approaches to investing. There may be a particular approach that is more suited to your personality and goals.

Let's start with the difference between investing and trading.

INVESTING VS. TRADING

Trading and investing are two distinct and very different things. By my definition, *investing* involves putting away money to earn a return over five, ten, or even twenty years and beyond. Investors have the patience to buy a stock based on a company's business fundamentals and not track its price movement for many days or maybe even months at a time. Investors have the fortitude to stay steady through bull markets, when the market as a whole is climbing, and through bear markets, when values can drop 20% or more. They don't panic. This long-term approach is often called a *buy-and-hold strategy*, which simply means buying a stock with the intention of holding it for many years. (Warren Buffett says his favorite holding period for a stock is "forever.") In this way, we defer capital gains tax until we choose to sell.

Trading, by contrast, is focused on the price of the stock and its daily movement. Traders are more concerned with the stock's price in the short run than with what the company actually does to earn a profit, and they are likely to be technicians, meaning they follow the chart of the historical price movement of a stock to assess when to buy and sell. In a nutshell, traders don't care if a stock is fairly valued—they just care whether it is moving in their favor. Traders have a shorter attention span and shorter time requirement for an expected return than investors do. Patience is not a virtue for traders. (Sounds a little like our Gambler personality, doesn't it?)

Day-trading typically means owning a stock (or stock options) for less than a day. That can mean a few hours, or even milliseconds, within a trading day. (Read Michael Lewis's *Flash Boys* for fascinating insight.) Robinhood is a free trading platform that started in 2015 and really caught fire in 2020. It has a mobile interface and no minimum deposit requirements, making it easy to get started buying and selling stocks, ETFs, REITs (real estate investment trusts), and cryptocurrency. It's so easy, in fact, that a lot of folks have jumped into trading simply for entertainment value—Robinhood has, in essence, "gamified" trading. To me, most of it is merely online gambling, exacerbated by the pandemic, for folks looking for a new thrill.

Frequent trading leads to high portfolio turnover. I find it challenging enough to choose the right stock the *first* time. Constantly selling and immediately buying something else turns that one big decision into three needing to be made in short succession: the first buy, the timing on the sell, and then another buy. Why not instead do your homework and live with the fact that, in the long run, the stock you choose will be just fine and at least track with its industry and thus the overall market? If you want to be a trader and think you're good enough, then by all means go for it, but realize it's like going to the Bellagio poker room in Vegas and expecting to beat Johnny Chan.

You may also hear of an approach called *momentum investing*, which involves following market trends: riding the wave up and knowing exactly when to get off. The trend may be short, or it could be quite long, but this strategy tends to be closer to trading than to investing, because it relies more on technical data and price movement than it does on the companies' fundamental value and potential.

In case I haven't been clear, I am a fan of the buy-and-hold investment strategy—I'm in it for the long term—and my advice is targeted in that direction. Next let's look at active versus passive investing, both of which could be used in long-term investing.

ACTIVE INVESTING VS. PASSIVE INVESTING

Active investing simply means that you (or someone you hire) are actively making decisions in an attempt to beat the stock market average as measured by an index like the S&P 500. Active investing could include selecting an individual company's stock for inclusion in your portfolio. It could also include choosing between several professionally managed mutual funds.

Mutual fund assets are typically managed by an individual or a team of managers (an *active manager*) whose job is to stay true to their investing style (see the next section). Regardless of their focus, active managers are trying to outperform the market in that arena.

In contrast, *passive investing* means we forego a professional stock picker and simply let the overall market returns become our own. We are "buying the market" and accepting the returns in a "passive" manner. For example, we may invest in an ETF that represents the whole market using an index like the Russell 3000. In this way our return will be fully correlated to the overall market, less the fees charged, which are extremely low. We are fully diversified since we are buying and tracking the entire market. This is sometimes called *index investing*. (Incidentally, recognize that about 20 percent of the S&P 500 is composed of what's known as the FAANG stocks—Meta-owned Facebook, Amazon, Apple, Netflix, and Alphabet-owned Google—so you may not be as diversified as you think.)

You say you want to beat the market? Me too. So why would you choose to invest passively? Because active fund managers tend to underperform against the market in any given year— 80 percent of them underperformed in 2021![26] Thus, low-cost ETFs and passive mutual funds that track whatever the market does have become popular. If the pros can't beat the market consistently, some people figure they might as well take what the market gives them. Also, think about the time and engagement level needed for these two types of investing: with passive, you can buy and let the market do its thing; with active, you (or the fund manager) need to put a little more effort into choosing your investments up front and pay closer attention to them on a regular basis.

INVESTING STYLES

There are two major styles of investing—value and growth. (Note you may hear the terms *strategy* and *style* used interchangeably, but I think of strategy as a general philosophy like buy-and-hold and a style as a specific focus.)

In *value investing*, you focus on purchasing undervalued stocks. The idea is that you are buying before everyone else realizes how great the company is, when the stock does not yet reflect the company's performance or potential. Once the market eventually has its eyes opened, the price will increase to the stock's "real" value, thus giving you a good return. (Shoppers, this is a great area in which to deploy your good-deal skills.)

Intel Corporation is a good example of a value stock. I bought some of its shares at $20 back in 2011; it had a dividend yield of 3.5% and was trading with a price-to-earnings ratio of only 10 (more on this ratio is coming up). *The Value Line Investment Survey* showed it with a strong financial strength rating (A++) with very steady earnings. To me, it looked like a strong, industry-leading company at a great price. With my patient buy-and-hold mentality, I got paid over 3% per year as I waited for the stock to move up. It reached a pre-pandemic high of $67, and I have no doubt that it will do well in the future.

By contrast, in *growth investing*, you are looking for stocks that have the potential to outperform the market over time. This often means investing in start-ups or newer companies that appear to have a potentially superior trajectory compared to other companies in their sector. Keep in mind that younger companies have less of a track record, so growth investing can entail higher risk than value investing.

One of the best growth stocks our family has ever owned is Dollar Tree. Dollar Tree is a well-known retailer, recognized by everyone, and has a simple business model that anyone can understand: sell things for a dollar. We purchased shares in 2008 when there were about 3,500 stores with sales of $4.64 billion. Today Dollar Tree has over 15,000 stores with annual sales of over $25 billion—that's a lot of $1 items! A stock we purchased at $8 per share was worth north of $140 per share by 2022. That's some serious growth.

Value and growth are the core investing styles, but there are also blends of them, and there's plenty of blurriness across categories. As you start reading about investing, you'll find lists out there with four styles or nine styles, or various sub-styles of value and growth. For example, *small-cap* refers to companies with a smaller market capitalization (a company's *market valuation*, or *market capitalization*, is simply the number of shares of stock outstanding times the price per share), thus "small-cap." *Large-cap* refers to companies with large market capitalization, and *mid-cap* is of course in the middle. Small-cap companies tend to be younger and are generally considered growth stocks. Large-cap companies are more mature and thus likely to be value stocks. Mutual funds as well can be labeled by style, so the fund manager's job is to make sure they stick to the style intended.

Some people consider momentum investing a style, but we'll set that aside as more of a trading approach since it doesn't focus on business fundamentals. My advice: don't get tangled up in terminology about investing styles and strategy; just try to focus on the intent of the approach and what you want to achieve.

STRATEGICALLY TIMED PURCHASES VS.
DOLLAR-COST AVERAGING

One more thing to consider is how you want to put money into your investments. Do you want to invest a large lump sum in something? Or do you want to invest a little bit at a time?

Putting in small amounts of money on a regular schedule is called *dollar-cost averaging*. You buy every week or every month regardless of the price, with the assumption that you'll get a good deal over time. For example, if you have a portion of every paycheck deposited into your 401(k), you are using dollar-cost averaging.

This term can also be used to describe a short series of scheduled purchases. For example, if a company has a profit-sharing program that puts money in employees' accounts at year-end (similar to a 401(k) match), the investment-related payments may be made in multiple tranches (installments). When the money goes into the employees' accounts, it purchases whatever funds the employees have selected; using multiple tranches helps minimize the risk of buying at an anomalously high price on one day.

Dollar-cost averaging is a great approach for your retirement funds; however, when you are at the top of the wealth-building pyramid, it may be better to look for opportunities to make strategically timed purchases (and certainly you can do both). My opinion has always been that you can't time the market. However, you *can* wait for a good entry point—like March 2020 when the market dropped due to the initial impact of the pandemic—and then buy investments "on sale" intending to hold them for the long term. Making strategic purchases like this requires patience and discipline: you need to know what you want to purchase and pay close enough attention to do so when the opportunity presents itself. And you need to store up some funds—called "keeping some dry powder"—for when the next correction comes along.

TYPES OF EQUITY INVESTMENTS

Now that you've considered possible approaches for your investing, it's time to look at specific types of equity investments. We have several choices to get started. By far the most common way to invest is through the indirect ownership of common stocks through mutual funds or exchange-traded funds (ETFs).

MUTUAL FUNDS

Mutual funds are the de facto standard in the investment world today. A *mutual fund* is a collection of investments, such as stocks or bonds, of which individual investors own a portion. A fund manager decides what goes into the fund and manages it on an ongoing basis, and all the investors in the fund experience the same return from their collective investment.

Because of their structure, mutual funds are extremely efficient at spreading risk and have become the individual investor's most convenient and flexible way to invest their savings in the stock market. Almost everyone with a retirement account holds some mutual funds. And even if you invest only a modest amount, it is diversified by the choices of a professional fund manager or through the purchase of the entire market through an index fund. (Recall from Chapter 7 that diversification lowers your risk relative to an individual stock.)

As mentioned above, there is a focus to the fund's investments, a style such as growth or value (or a substyle like small-cap or mid-cap). Funds must report their top ten holdings every quarter, but since it is always after the fact, you may not know precisely what stocks are held (though you can make some reasonable suppositions based on historical information).

When investing in an actively managed mutual fund, you are at the mercy of the fund manager for your fund's ultimate performance (return). And investing in last year's mutual fund star is a bit like fishing—you should have been there yesterday. So a mutual fund is a great starting point for all of us, but, for the most part, you are buying a pool of stocks that over time will likely perform much like the market does.

EXCHANGE-TRADED FUNDS (ETFS)

Exchange-traded funds (ETFs) are similar to mutual funds in that they are collections of securities that usually track an index, sector, or other asset. Both trade based on their *net asset value (NAV)*, which is the per-unit price. However, an ETF trades like a stock throughout the trading day, whereas a mutual fund trades off the NAV determined at the *end* of the trading day.

ETFs have grown in popularity over the last few years for passive investors and tend to be a little more cost-effective than mutual funds. For the long-term investor, however, you shouldn't get too caught up in the differences, as either one can work well. Focus instead on the cost of the mutual fund or ETF when making your decision to invest.

Full disclosure: Like most people, I hold mutual funds in my retirement plan, but for my self-directed accounts, I've never bought mutual funds or ETFs. I have always felt it's a lot more intriguing and interesting to own individual stocks directly through a brokerage account. You know what business you're invested in and you can watch the company grow (hopefully) over time. So let's look at individual stocks . . .

INDIVIDUAL STOCKS

Stocks represent equity, or ownership, in a company. With a mutual fund or ETF, you have a basket of often-unknown investments, but with a stock, you can familiarize yourself with the products and services a specific company sells, as well as how it competes in its industry and marketplace.

Earlier we looked at two major styles of investing: growth and value. Correspondingly, individual stocks are often categorized as a *growth stock* or a *value stock* (or they may be newly listed as a startup and not have a clear categorization beyond that).

As we know from earlier discussion, value investors look for stocks that are undervalued based on their fundamentals. A value stock is often older and more established, and it often pays a dividend to its shareholders. For example, Dow Inc. (you probably know its subsidiary Dow Chemical) has been around in some form since 1897. It pays quarterly dividends and has shown consistent but slow growth in dividends over time. Dividend-paying stocks are also referred to as *income stocks* (they could be value stocks but don't necessarily have to be undervalued).

With growth stocks we are more interested in capital appreciation if and when the company is successful in executing its strategy. Growth companies typically reinvest all of their profits back into the company for further growth, thereby foregoing paying much in the way of dividends (if any). For example, Amazon plows all of its earnings back into its growth plans, so you would buy it for appreciation, not for dividends.

Although it's desirable to have a blend of income and appreciation, there is nothing wrong with holding a pure value stock or a pure growth stock.

I prefer individual stocks over mutual funds and ETFs for several reasons:

1. Stocks have real earnings attached to their price, which can be monitored via their quarterly earnings performance (more on this in the next section on choosing stocks).

2. By owning stock, you have direct ownership in a company rather than owning only "the market" or even a fund that invests in other funds (a so-called "fund of funds").

3. With stocks, you have much better potential to take advantage of market corrections—that is, to buy low when the next correction occurs (and it will occur) and reap subsequent gains. (Read *A Random Walk Down Wall Street* or *The Intelligent Investor*.)

4. With stocks, you have greater control over paying capital gains tax. With an actively traded mutual fund, at the end of the year you receive a 1099 tax statement from the fund company with capital gains listed, even if you didn't sell any shares, because the fund manager sold stocks held in the fund, thus generating capital gains. As a stock owner, on the other hand, you get to decide when to sell and incur capital gains. Additionally, for tax purposes you may want to offset capital gains

with losses—a process known as *tax harvesting* that is typically done in December before the end of the tax year; however, with mutual funds you don't know what the gains will be, so this offset process becomes more difficult.

5. Both mutual funds and stocks will appreciate (you hope); however, with stocks you may be more likely to get a "large gainer." If you do, and you want to avoid taxes on that gain, you can use that stock as a way to donate to your favorite charity. For example, if a $5,000 investment in Lowe's Home Improvement turns into $50,000, you have a nice $45,000 capital gain that would be taxed if you sold the shares. By donating the stock (transferring the shares directly to the charity), they get the full $50,000 value, with no negative tax consequences for either party. You get the full $50,000 tax deduction as well. (This transfer approach can be used with mutual funds too, but the likelihood of a large gainer, and thus the benefit of the approach, is greater with stocks.)

6. With individual securities, the personal interest you take in your stock portfolio increases sharply, especially if you selected the stock yourself, and you build investment confidence over time. It is much more interesting to follow the stock of Apple than it is a generic SPDR (pronounced "spider," standing for Standard & Poor's Depository Receipt) mutual fund. Following the performance of a company whose stock you own is not unlike following your favorite sports team. It can be a lot of fun to watch the value of your investment increase over time.

■■■

Peter Lynch was one of the best mutual fund investment managers of all time. His Fidelity Magellan Fund had a value of only $18 million in assets when he assumed management in 1977. By 1990, the fund had grown to $14 billion in value with an average annual return of nearly 30%, and by 2003, it had enjoyed the best twenty-year run of any mutual fund in history.

In 1988, Lynch wrote the classic *One Up on Wall Street.* The book offers great advice for the beginning investor by explaining how to search for good companies that would make a great stock investment. By observing a good business with attractive growth prospects, he reasoned that anyone could participate in the stock market. (Remember that not all good companies make a good stock holding.) Lynch coined terms such as "growth at a reasonable price" (a.k.a. GARP) and "ten-bagger" stocks (meaning a stock that reached ten times its original price, a baseball analogy for the number of bases run, e.g., a home run is a four-bagger). Lynch taught us to invest in what we were familiar with, not unlike Warren Buffett, who famously shied away from tech stocks for many years because he didn't understand them or couldn't explain to his shareholders what the business did.

In a nutshell, you had Peter Lynch, the greatest mutual fund guy of all time, writing a book telling us to invest in individual stocks! So let's look at how to start choosing individual stocks to invest in.

CHOOSING INDIVIDUAL STOCKS

At this point, you've decided that at least a portion of your investments will be self-directed in individual stocks, and you've considered whether you're more interested in growth or value investing or both. Congratulations on thinking through all that!

Now, for each individual stock pick, you'll want to decide if you want income (dividends) or appreciation (growth) or both, and then research the underlying metrics that show it's a good company.

PRICE-TO-EARNINGS RATIO

Determining what a stock is worth (or what it *should* be worth) is the critical art of the investing world. There are computer models galore that can crunch the data and spit out what an advisor thinks a stock is worth. There are more metrics than I can count for assessing every aspect of a company and its stock. There are countless analysts who study one industry and attempt to make a prediction of future value. But there is no perfect, foolproof valuation method.

However, by far the most useful and dependable metric is the *price-to-earnings ratio* (often abbreviated *P/E ratio* or just *P/E* or *PE*). The P/E ratio divides the company's current stock price by its *earnings per share* (*EPS*). EPS is profit over a particular period of time divided by shares outstanding. So if Acme Company currently sells for $30 per share and its *forward earnings*—that is, its estimated future earnings—for the next twelve months are $3 per share, then the P/E of Acme equals 10, expressed either as ratio (share price ÷ earnings per share = $30 ÷ $3 = 10) or as a multiple of its earnings ($3 EPS × 10 = $30 share price). If the stock doubles in price to $60 per share, then the P/E ratio (also called the *multiple*) increases to 20, assuming earnings don't change.

What is a reasonable P/E ratio? Great question. No one can

really answer that, because the market will go through periods when it rewards stocks overall with historically high P/Es or, vice versa, penalizes them with low P/Es. This is certainly where the *art* of investing, through much experience and knowledge, comes in. But we can look at stocks' historical P/Es to know a reasonable P/E ratio is in the range of 10 to 20. Generally speaking, growth companies can usually justify a higher price-to-earnings ratio than others due to their faster growth. A company that is growing its earnings by, say, 10% or more per year likely merits a higher P/E ratio—maybe even 30 or more. In essence, if a company has a higher P/E, it means that investors think the company will have faster earnings growth than a company with a lower P/E.

The P/E ratio helps us keep in perspective the price we are paying for each dollar of current earnings. If we buy stock of a company with a P/E of 12, we are paying $12 for every dollar of current earnings. So if, for example, we observe a stock with a historical multiple around 18 and the market gives us a chance to buy the stock when the multiple is only 10, which indicates it may be undervalued, we should be successful with our individual stock investment over time (if we practice patience).

However, Peter Lynch taught us that even if growth stocks are what we are after, we still must be mindful of obtaining that growth at a reasonable price (GARP). Without regard to a reasonable P/E ratio, a stock price can get out of hand quickly. Tesla is a good case study. If you had bought Tesla stock and owned it for just the year 2020, in at about $28 and out at about $235, you would have had an eight-bagger return. This is basically a form of momentum investing, riding the acceleration of a growth company. But when we do this, we decouple the price-to-earnings relationship completely.

Look at Tesla's P/E. To start 2020, the P/E ratio was not applicable (often shown as 0), because Tesla's earnings were negative. By the end of 2020, Tesla's P/E was over 1,100— extraordinarily high. When we buy stock with a P/E like this, we are paying a high price and betting completely on growth and profits down the road. Things could work out fine for Tesla, but if earnings do not materialize, the stock price becomes subject to a lot of volatility and could adjust downward quickly. In fact, by mid-2022, Tesla's P/E was back down around 80—still high but not stratospheric.

Basing a stock's value on its future earnings stream is, for me, the truer way to value the shares of a company. A stock with a track record of profitability and with a reasonable multiple at least has a proven measure of value connected to real earnings. Although imperfect, the P/E is the best metric we have at our disposal to value what we believe a company may be worth. A company with a reasonable P/E ratio at least has a metric to keep the price within a narrower range, which reduces your risk.

In time, you will learn to consider some of the other common metrics in deciding on investments, but for now, the P/E is key and will keep you focused on companies making money tethered to something real.

RESOURCES FOR DECIDING WHERE TO INVEST

Recall we talked earlier about triangulation—finding at least three sources of solid information to help you make a financial decision more objectively. The same guideline applies to selecting stocks. By using at least three sources of information, you can triangulate your reasoning as to why you think the stock is a good investment. All sources should answer yes as to whether the stock meets your criteria. This is also where the art of investing comes in, because you can study numbers and financials all day long, but that won't give you the intangibles that are needed to make the decision. Sometimes it's a gut call whether to buy or not, but that intuition is strengthened by patience and experience.

Here are some of the places I go to learn more about stocks I am interested in investing in.

Value Line. My all-time favorite resource is *The Value Line Investment Survey*. Value Line (VL) has been around since 1931 as the best independent source for stock information. You won't ever find advertising on their site or within the survey itself. It has stayed true to its roots nearly to a fault and has a dependable, straightforward, no-nonsense style, sort of like pulling out the classic tuxedo for a formal event—it's the same for everyone and has been forever. Value Line's large green binder was legendary in the days before the internet, when many investors would go to their local library to look up stocks of interest.

The survey includes about 1,700 stocks, representing about 90 percent of US trading volume. Each stock has its own page packed with information and data, and the report is updated each quarter. Value Line is my primary source and starting point when I am considering a new investment. Yes, there are unlimited other sources out there with even more detailed information; however, are they trying to sell you something? Is it teaser information to get you to sign up for a monthly fee? Is the analyst independent? Are you sure?

At a price of about $600 per year, Value Line could be the best investment you'll ever make. Sometimes I use Value Line as my only source for making an initial investment in a stock; that in itself tells you the kind of confidence I have in it. However, routinely I use VL as my base for getting the initial background on a company and then move on to other sources to go further in depth.

Online Investment Sites. Once Value Line has provided me solid foundational information, I can take the next step and look online for more information on the stock to get a real sense of their future prospects. Sites I visit regularly include:

- Morningstar
- S&P Global (Standard & Poor's)
- Kiplinger
- The Motley Fool
- The Wall Street Journal
- Barron's
- Investor's Business Daily

Give yourself time to get familiar with these websites and what they provide. The volume of information may be overwhelming at first, but your learning will pick up speed considerably, provided you stay with it. You'll learn to start asking questions like:

- Is the company making money?
- Does the company pay dividends? If so, what is the yield?
- How much debt does the company have?
- What is the financial strength rating?

While Value Line provides a lot of this basic information and compares the stock to a universe of choices, you'll also develop your own particular areas of focus you like to understand in greater depth.

Additionally, you might like to see what the industry analysts are saying. The platform where you have your brokerage account (see Trading Platforms section below) likely provides access to various analyst reports, especially for larger companies, which of course get more coverage than smaller companies. (For this reason, smaller companies tend to be riskier because they are less scrutinized.) However, be cautious when analysts make buy/sell recommendations. Do your own research and make your own decisions. And it bears repeating: Look for unbiased information and watch out for ads.

Company Websites. After checking at least two sources (including Value Line) for a potential stock purchase, I finally go to the company's website to review their annual report and get a picture of the markets in which the company competes. One word of caution, and part of the reason I don't go here first: companies (nearly all of them) are infamous for their glossy annual reports, so beware of an overly pretentious style. Look out for "spin"; focus on fundamentals. Besides the annual report, also check companies' Investor Relations pages; you can often find valuable investor presentations there.

Try to get an overall feel for the strength and scope of the company and whether they are the number one or two player in the market in which they compete. Make sure you have an interest in the business they are in and that the company matches up with your values. There have been many times I've looked back at an investment and thought, "What was I thinking?" One time in my early twenties, I bought stock from a friend who had a "hot" stock tip. The company name implied they were international thoroughbred horse breeders, but in actuality they owned and leased racetracks in New Jersey. I made almost every mistake possible: I bought a stock I knew nothing about; I didn't care anything about horses *or* racetracks; I had only one source of information (my friend); and the purchase entailed single-stock risk (recall that one stock is riskier than a diversified portfolio of stocks). I wanted to help my friend, but I should have known better, and the stock ended up being worthless. Luckily, I hadn't invested too much.

Business TV Shows. Are business TV shows good sources of investment advice? Well, I'll admit: I enjoy watching CNBC's *Halftime Report* at lunchtime. The show does a good job of keeping you abreast of the market news for the day. With names like The Judge, Farmer Jim, Doc Najarian, Downtown Josh Brown, and Mr. Wonderful (from *Shark Tank*), it stands to reason that these guys are entertaining. However, I'm not sure who their real audience is or should be. As my good friend and registered investment adviser once commented: "We in the business refer to those shows as financial porn—it may be fun to look at, but it's probably not good for you."

These shows (not just *Halftime*) are always making stock recommendations and giving advice, but the average viewer would have a hard time determining if the commentators were advising to hold the stock for a month, or for several years. The host will say they are a long-term investor and then in the next breath, they will mention a trade they just made. They truly are all active traders or momentum investors. Sort of like a freight train, they are looking to hop on as it accelerates and then hop off when it starts to slow down. When you tie your whole strategy to the movement of the stock price only, that can turn stock investing into pure trading decoupled from earnings (as discussed above).

Take Peloton as an example. During the pandemic they were all the rage since everyone was stuck at home craving a new workout experience. Sales went through the roof. But remember, we are evaluating the stock, not the company, and not every great company makes a great stock holding—a company may fall out of favor (when the fad is over) and/or its price-to-earnings ratio may be way too inflated. So if we are evaluating a company on its future earnings potential, we must ask: Has the ship already sailed?

In January 2020, pre-pandemic, Peloton was trading at about $28 per share and had a market capitalization of about $8 billion. In early January 2021, the share price was around $152 and the market cap had risen to nearly $45 billion. If you had gotten on the momentum train early, you could have had a five-bagger, but a year into the pandemic, should you buy the stock?

As a value investor who keeps an eye on the price paid for a stock based on its future earnings, I would look at the P/E ratio. In November 2020 the EPS was $0.20, very low, giving us a P/E of over 700, extremely high. Prior to that, the EPS was negative. The estimated (future) EPS was $0.10, again giving us an extremely high P/E ratio. I would have advised not to buy. Sure enough, by late 2022, Peloton was trading at under $10 per share.

You'll hear CNBC continue to talk about stocks like this all the time. They jump on the momentum train, but at the first sign of a problem, they jump right back off and move on to talk about the next hot stock investment. It's not difficult to see why folks can struggle trying to choose a solid stock when most of the recommendations coming at them are just not right for the individual investor. However, if we start with a staid but consistent and unbiased source like Value Line, it can keep us grounded and help us look at a company's intrinsic value based on its fundamentals.

Staying grounded is important in investing; we want to take a lot of the emotion out. Seth Klarman noted in his book *Margin of Safety*, "Unsuccessful investors are dominated by emotion. . . . [They] regard the stock market as a way to make money without working rather than as a way to invest capital in order to earn a decent return." Our American get-rich-quick, Gold Rush–type mentality can help us dream big, but it can also make us impatient. As Klarman further notes, "Greed can cause investors to shift their focus away from the achievement of long-term investment goals in favor of short-term speculation."

The successful investor has the ability and temperament to stay patient and focus on the long term; they take bear markets and corrections in stride without panic. The smart ones keep some cash available so when the market does correct 20 percent (or even more), they can buy stock "on sale." They thus increase their chances of following the golden rule of investing—"buy low and sell high"—which most investors fail to do, since they act on emotion and listen to FFF (friends, family, and fools) instead of doing their own research and using solid data.

Overall, feel free to enjoy the business TV shows, but use other sources for decision-making.

A SUGGESTED APPROACH FOR NEW INVESTORS

It can feel overwhelming to get started—there are so many options. Here is the type of approach I would suggest for new investors . . .

First, have a pool of funds in very safe stocks known for their consistent track record of paying dividends. Generally speaking, a company that pays steady dividends must be able to fund the payouts through a consistent stream of earnings (profits). The advantage here is that you can get started investing in the market a bit more gently. There are many "steady Eddie" companies that can pay you 2% or more per year, not including the opportunity for stock price (capital) appreciation. The total return (dividend yield plus stock appreciation) in a given year can be quite compelling and a great way to earn a return over the rate of inflation without taking on a huge amount of risk. In other words, moving some idle money out of savings or CDs into a portfolio of dividend-paying stocks can be an excellent strategy to construct your beginning portfolio.

Next, you might consider a growth company that will "take flight" over the coming years. (Take a long-term view to allow plenty of time for the company to grow into their business plan, else you will fall into the category of a trader.) Any time you observe a great business with a great business model, you can jump in as an owner to share in the profits. As for me, I rode past ULTA, a popular chain of beauty stores, every day for years and never pulled the trigger. If I had only paid attention, I would have had a ten-bagger in ten years!

That's it. Start there. Take your time, do your research, and gain confidence to decide what's next.

As you progress, there's a lot more to learn. Two topics I suggest you read about sooner rather than later: asset allocation and portfolio rebalancing. *Asset allocation* is the ratio you choose for investing your money in different assets. It's basically the pie chart of your investments, and it's an important consideration for your portfolio. Long-term investors are often in the range of 70% stocks, 25% bonds, and 5% cash. However, even if you start with that allocation, over time it will get out of balance as the investments grow at different rates.

Portfolio rebalancing is just what it sounds like—periodically getting your investment portfolio back into your intended asset allocation by buying or selling the appropriate assets. When rebalancing back to your target allocation, what you are really doing is selling some of the winners and buying some of the losers. This is you buying low and selling high! Also, you are shifting back to the overall risk level you originally intended.

TRADING PLATFORMS

One question you might have is "Where do I actually go to buy stock??" In a nutshell, you go to one of any number of online trading platforms and open a brokerage account. (In this case, "trading" means "performing transactions," not being a trader or a day trader.) Some of the platform names might be familiar to you: Fidelity Investments, TD Ameritrade, Charles Schwab, Vanguard, eTrade.

I am not making a specific suggestion—I am platform-agnostic—but here are some things to consider as you look for the platform that's right for you:

- Do they offer the types of investments you want to invest in? (For example, some platforms may not offer options. But I don't suggest you start there anyway.)
- Do they charge for transactions, or are those free?
- What are their other fees (for example, fund fees if you are interested in mutual funds)?
- What types of research and resources are included in the platform?

There are plenty of resources online to identify and assess possible platforms, so just do your homework.

WHEN IT'S TIME TO SELL

We've mentioned that one of the benefits of owning individual stocks is that you have control over when you sell or transfer the stock, which lets you manage those transactions in a way that is beneficial to your tax bill. Everyone's situation is different, so always be sure to talk to your tax advisor about the most advantageous time to sell and to make transfers.

Setting taxes aside, as you consider sales, here are a couple of trite but true pieces of advice . . .

- "Buy low, sell high." Yes, that's how you make money.
- "Ride the winners, sell the losers." If your stocks are climbing, hang onto them. If they're in decline, it might be time to let them go.

Those two pieces of advice might sound like they contradict each other. They don't. They just apply at different times, and, to be honest, determining which time is which is part of the art of investing. Learning the difference will come from experience and a few good mistakes along the way. This is how we grow as investors.

For example, when stocks perform well, over time they can become too large a portion of your portfolio, throwing your asset allocation out of balance. As mentioned previously, you may need to rebalance your portfolio by selling some stock to bring things back into balance. As a general guideline, if you find that one stock makes up 10 percent or more of your portfolio, it's probably time to rebalance, reducing that percentage to keep your risk diversified. That is, you may want to sell some of that stock and take the gain in order to reduce that holding. (Sell high.)

But by far the biggest problem I see is the tendency for people to hang onto stock *too long*. We get attached to our "team." We think the underdog can always come back to win. Besides, we already spent money buying the stock—we have to recoup our cost at least, right? It's easy to get caught in the sunk cost fallacy, making emotional decisions based on past expenditures rather than rational forward-looking decisions.

Take my adventure with Blackberry. Those of us in business thought this device, which could deliver our emails to our phone (wow!), was the greatest thing since, well, the internet. I rode it all the way up to $146/share in 2007–2008. Then Apple introduced the iPhone, and the rest was history. I foolishly held onto my Blackberry stock and rode it back down to $10 a share instead of selling when it became a loser. Moral of the story: Take the profit. (A two-bagger in three years is not too shabby.)

Don't try to time the market, don't try to get the biggest possible profit, and don't try to recoup losses on a stock that will never come back. When possible, hold your stock for the long haul, but don't let greed crowd your thinking. If you see things turning downward and you think it is permanent, there is no shame in taking a profit and paying some taxes. But if the business and industry remain viable, you are in a great position to hold that stock for the very long term.

ARE YOU READY TO START INVESTING?

The key to stock market investing and the main point I would like to make is this: For most of us, it's about just getting in the game. That's it. Don't get hung up on your returns and how you tracked with the market. That in itself is difficult since any benchmark used is merely a guide anyway. There are a lot of paths to having a successful journey in the market. The real secret is getting in the game and staying in the game.

Get started today. Learn. Study. Act. All of your hard-earned savings sitting in a bank account earning near zero interest is the *real* risk. Inflation risk is real, and the US stock market is the best game in town with the most proven track record in the most proven economy.

I began investing when I was twelve years old. I've lost money on occasion, but by doing regular research and paying attention to the fundamentals, I've made much more than I've lost, and I've created financial security for my family. You can too.

CONCLUSION

PLAN CAREFULLY AND YOU WILL HAVE
PLENTY; IF YOU ACT TOO QUICKLY, YOU
WILL NEVER HAVE ENOUGH.
—PROVERBS 21:5 (GNT)

OUR CAPITALIST SOCIETY encourages us to seize the moment and spend, spend, spend, and our latest toys and gadgets are far more interesting to talk about over drinks than saving and budgeting are. Yet we need to have a conversation wherein we do discuss what we value, because this can be the first step towards developing the financial discipline necessary to secure our futures. Common sense alone won't cut it. To build security and wealth, we must increase our financial literacy, manage our emotions so we develop good money habits, and follow a plan.

Building wealth takes patience, as we use time to take advantage of compound interest. With an environment of low interest rates and high inflation, traditional bank savings will simply not suffice to meet our ultimate goal of financial independence. Once we have a solid financial foundation, investing in the stock market can give us the flexibility to achieve our wealth goals faster by putting the odds of a large return in our favor. If we can reach somewhere near the top of the Wealth Pyramid, we then become financially secure enough to free ourselves from the constant worry of all things money. We can become financially independent and not be a burden on our family. Our children and successive generations can then inherit a lasting legacy that benefits them directly, but better yet, we can create and accomplish our own philanthropic goals to make a better society. The choices are unlimited—through your faith community or other charitable endeavors—to help secure a better future for all succeeding generations.

I hope I have convinced you that making sense of money and taking control of your personal finances is possible and that it can ease your anxiety about money matters. The concepts covered in this book are my best practices to help you get started. No matter our income, background, or IQ, there are always areas that we can improve on—no one ever fully masters this stuff. The key is simply to take action.

As I look back on my own financial journey, I am again reminded how lucky I was to have grandparents who were frugal and financially disciplined in good times and bad. I am again reminded how lucky I am that my parents continued that pattern, that I learned about finances and investing growing up, and that I benefited from the legacy I was given in the family business.

And as I look forward to the next generation, I hope I am creating in my children that same understanding of personal finance. I am pleased when my son asks great questions about getting started with investing. Although he may view the world a bit differently than my wife and I do, we can see the progress he's made over the years in becoming responsible with money. Likewise, it is gratifying to see that my daughter is well prepared to make her own money decisions as she steps out into the business world. Her maturation process throughout the college years has been fun to observe as she develops her own money personality. I hope both will be able to carry on the family tradition of being savers and investors, and leave their own legacies.

You may not have had the upbringing I did, but we all have the ability to improve our own lives and those of future generations. It starts with financial discipline, and it might entail some sacrifice, but as you look at the next generation and your legacy, isn't it worth it?

FINANCIAL AND INVESTING TERMS

Basic definitions are provided for terms used throughout this book. However, many of these terms have more in-depth technical definitions, so when you're ready, do more reading!

529 Plan. A tax-advantaged vehicle to save money for education expenses, typically for college.

Active Investing. An investment approach in which you (or a manager) are actively trying to beat the market. Compare to *passive investing*.

Active Manager. The individual or team that manages an investment such as a mutual fund, making buy and sell decisions while keeping true to the fund's intended style.

Adjustable-Rate Mortgage (ARM). A mortgage in which the interest rate changes periodically, usually on an annual basis. The risk comes when you have an initial low rate and then the rate jumps significantly (possibly to the point you can't afford it).

Advisor-Managed Investing. Using a professional to manage your investments. Compare to *self-directed investing*.

Alternative Investment. An *investment* that does not fall into the traditional investment categories of stocks and bonds. Alternatives include things like gold, silver, options, futures, and cryptocurrency.

Amortization. How loan payments get applied to principal and interest each month over the life of a loan. For example, with most mortgages, even if the payment is the same, initially a large portion goes towards interest; over time a larger portion goes towards principal.

Analyst. Someone who studies the market and individual companies and provides analysis and advice. There are a number of different types of analysts, such as buy-side, sell-side, financial, and research.

Annuity. A financial product in which you pay one lump sum up front in return for a series of payments over time. Annuities have many variations and can be quite complex.

Appreciate. To grow in value. Typically, investments are expected to appreciate or at least have a good chance of appreciation.

Asset. Anything with present or future value; it may lose value (*depreciate*) or gain value (*appreciate*).

Asset Allocation. Asset allocation is the ratio you choose for investing your money in different assets, such as stocks, bonds, and cash. See also *portfolio rebalancing.*

Balance Sheet. A business financial statement that shows a company's assets, liabilities, and owners' equity, represented as: assets = liabilities – owners' equity (or as owner's equity = assets – liabilities). Similar to a *personal financial statement (PFS)* showing net worth.

Balloon Mortgage. A mortgage in which you have a low payment (sometimes interest only) for a period of time and then must pay the principal in full (often through refinancing).

Bear Market. When the stock market as a whole drops precipitously, typically 20% or more. Compare to *bull market.*

Bond. A fixed-income investment. When you buy a bond, you are essentially giving a company or a government entity a long-term loan in return for interest payments, known as coupon payments, typically made twice a year. At the end date, the bonds mature and the principal becomes due. Compare to *stock*.

Brokerage Account. The account you create on a *trading platform* in order to make investment (e.g., stocks, bonds, mutual funds) purchases and sales.

Budget. An estimate of expected revenues (income) and expenses over a period of time, often a month or a year.

Bull Market. When the market as a whole is climbing, often 20% or more, especially after there have been steep declines. Compare to *bear market*.

Buy-and-Hold Strategy. An investing approach in which you purchase stocks with the intention of holding them for a significant time—five, ten, twenty years. Compare to *momentum investing*, *trading*, and *day-trading*.

Capital Gains. The amount you take in profit from the sale of an investment. While an investment may appreciate on paper, capital gains are realized only when a sale takes place. (And, yes, you could have a capital loss.)

Capital Gains Tax. The tax you pay when you sell an investment and realize a profit; you are taxed on the increase in value. If you've held the investment longer than a year, you pay the long-term capital gains tax rate, which is lower than the short-term capital gains tax rate. See also *capital gains*.

Cash Flow. Money flowing in and out, i.e., revenue and expenses, or income and expenditures. Positive cash flow means more is flowing in than out. Negative cash flow means more is flowing out than in.

Certificate of Deposit (CD). A financial instrument in which you deposit a sum of money at a bank or credit union for a set period of time, such as one year or five years, and receive an agreed-upon rate of interest.

Commodity. A type of good that is fungible; that is, it is basically the same coming from any producer. Examples include corn and soybeans, oil and natural gas, or gold and other metals.

Common Sense. Practical judgment derived primarily from experience rather than through study.

Compound Interest. Interest calculated on accumulated interest as well as on principal. Compound interest works for you over time on investments as they accumulate value. Conversely, if you have a loan that is accumulating interest, compound interest works against you by growing the amount you owe. Compare to *simple interest*.

Corporate Bond. A bond offered by a company. See also *bond*.

Coupon Payments. Interest payments on bonds, typically made twice a year.

Cryptocurrency. Cryptocurrency is a system to allow for secure payments online; it is valued as "virtual tokens." Bitcoin is the most well-known example.

Day-Trading. Owning a stock (or stock options) for a very short period of time, usually less than a day and sometimes a few hours or even milliseconds. Compare to *trading* and *investing*.

Debt. Something you owe; a liability.

Defined Benefit Plan. A plan in which an employer agrees to provide employees a certain benefit in retirement. A pension plan is the prime example of a defined benefit plan. Compare to *defined contribution plan*.

Defined Contribution Plan. A plan to which employees can contribute for retirement; employers may or may not make matching contributions. Two well-known examples of defined contribution plans are 401(k)s and 403(b)s. Compare to *defined benefit plan*.

Depreciate. To decrease in value. Assets may increase or decrease in value. Investments are assets typically expected to appreciate or at least have a good chance of appreciation; personal assets such as cars and furniture will almost always decrease in value.

Depression. A severe downturn in the economy, sometimes defined as a *recession* lasting three or more years or a decline in gross domestic product (GDP) of 10 percent in a given year.

Diversification. Diversification means having a variety of investments. Investing in a diversified mutual fund or index fund is typically safer than investing in a single stock. A portfolio constructed of many different stocks in many different industries can also give you much lower risk than a single stock.

Dividends/Stock Dividends. Payments made to shareholders on a regular basis, typically quarterly. Stocks that pay dividends are known as *income stocks*.

Dollar-Cost Averaging. Putting in small amounts of money on a regular schedule without regard to what the market is doing, e.g., regular 401(k) contributions from your paycheck. Compare to *strategic purchases*.

Earnings. How much a company makes, or its profits; often described in *earnings per share*.

Earnings Multiple. Also called *multiple*. Essentially the same as a *P/E ratio*. If XYZ stock has earnings of $10 per share and a stock price of $200 per share, it has a P/E ratio of 20. If the stock is selling for 20 times its earnings, its multiple is said to be 20.

Earnings Per Share (EPS). A company's profit during a given period divided by the number of shares outstanding.

Emergency Savings. A contingency fund for unexpected personal expenses; three to six months of salary is a commonly suggested amount to keep in this fund.

EPS. See *earnings per share*.

Equity. Ownership in something. Paying principal on your mortgage builds equity in your home; owning a company's stock means you have equity in that company. Stocks are often referred to as equities.

Exchange-Traded Fund (ETF). Collections of *securities* that usually track an index, sector, or other asset; an ETF trades on its *net asset value (NAV)* throughout the trading day. Compare to *mutual fund*.

FAANG Stocks. Facebook, Amazon, Apple, Netflix, Google. These stocks make up about 20 percent of the S&P 500.

Fiduciary. A fiduciary is legally bound to put their clients' interests ahead of their own.

Financial Discipline. In my definition, this entails gaining financial literacy, managing your money habits, and following a financial plan.

Flipping. Purchasing a house or other property to refurbish and resell quickly at a higher price.

Forward Earnings. Estimated future earnings (future profit). Often used in calculating an expected *EPS* and *P/E ratio*.

Frugality. Careful management of money; thriftiness.

Futures Contract. An agreement to buy or sell something on a specific date at a specific price. See also *options contract*.

Gambler (Money Personality). Someone who tends to spend a lot and take risks with their money; often too impatient to invest—they want a quick win. Compare to *investor, saver, shopper*, and *spendthrift*.

GARP. The concept of Growth At a Reasonable Price comes from Peter Lynch's *One Up on Wall Street*. The idea is to be mindful of the *P/E ratio* not getting too far out of whack; for example, if a company's historical P/E is 20, how is it now 50?

Growth Investing. Investing in stocks with an emphasis on appreciation in value. Compare to *income investing* and *value investing*.

Growth Stock. A stock that is expected to grow, possibly faster than the market. While growth stocks may pay dividends, most do not. Compare to *income stock* and *value stock*.

Hedging. Taking counteractions in case the market goes a different direction than you expect. *Futures* and *options* are often used for hedging.

Home Equity. The value of your ownership stake in your home, calculated by subtracting your mortgage balance from the house's market value.

Income. Money flowing in, e.g., from salary, wages, dividends, and/or interest.

Income Investing. Buying stocks that pay dividends providing a regular stream of income; real estate can also be an income investment. Compare to *growth investing*.

Income Stock. A stock that pays dividends on a regular basis, usually quarterly. Income stocks may also appreciate, but are purchased at least partly for the regular stream of payments. Compare to *growth stock* and *value stock*.

Inflation. An increase in price levels over a period of time. The consumer price index (CPI) is a common measure of inflation.

Inflation Rate. The rate at which prices are increasing. The average US annual inflation rate is around 4%.

Installment Loan. A loan in which a set amount of money is borrowed with a set repayment schedule; a *mortgage* is an installment loan.

Insurance. A policy purchased that provides a payout if certain events occur, e.g., a life insurance policy pays money upon the insured's death, and a disability policy pays a monthly payment if the insured is unable to work.

Interest. The money paid on a loan beyond the principal amount; the amount earned on an interest-paying investment. See also *principal*.

Intrinsic Value. A measure of what an asset is worth as de-termined by some objective calculation. For example, bonds have both an intrinsic value (the value of *coupon payments*) and a *market price* (what someone will buy a bond for based on movements in the interest rate market).

Investing. Allocating resources (money) with the expecta-tion of a return (*income* or *appreciation*) over time. By my defi-nition, investing involves buying a stock based on a company's business fundamentals and having the patience not to track its daily price movement.

Investing Style. A particular focus for an investment. The two major styles are *value* and *growth*; substyles include blends, small cap, large cap, and so on.

Investment. An *asset* that has the potential to and is expected to increase in value over time; common examples include stocks and mutual funds. Some investments may also contribute to return on investment (ROI) through income (e.g., interest, div-idends, rental income).

Investment Strategy. A general approach to investing, such as a *buy-and-hold* vs. a *momentum* strategy, or an *active* vs. a *passive* strategy.

Investor (Money Personality). Someone who tends to be fi-nancially literate and have good saving habits; they understand the need to grow their money at a rate faster than the inflation rate. Compare to *gambler, saver, shopper,* and *spendthrift.*

IRA/Traditional IRA/Roth IRA. Individual retirement ac-count. A traditional IRA is funded with pre-tax dollars, provid-ing a tax deduction immediately; taxes are paid on distributions in retirement. A Roth IRA is funded with after-tax dollars, and distributions can be taken tax-free in retirement.

Leverage. Increasing your purchasing power by using *debt*.

Liability. A *debt*; something you owe.

Liquidity. The ease with which an asset is converted to cash. Cash is the most liquid; stocks are very liquid (you can sell at almost any time); and real estate is one of the least liquid investments in that it can take a long time to sell.

Long-Term Investing. From a tax standpoint, holding an asset more than one year. From my viewpoint, using a time horizon of five years or more.

Market Capitalization. A company's stock price multiplied by the shares outstanding. Also known as *market valuation*.

Market Price. The price something sells for on the market, regardless of its intrinsic value. For example, bonds have both an *intrinsic value* (the value of coupon payments) and a market price (what someone will pay for a bond based on movements in the interest rate market).

Market Valuation. A company's stock price multiplied by the shares outstanding. Also known as *market capitalization*.

Maturity. The term to describe when a bond period expires and the principal is due.

Momentum Investing. An investing approach that involves following market trends: riding the wave up and knowing exactly when to get off. This strategy tends to be closer to trading than to investing, because it relies more on technical data and price movement than it does on the companies' fundamental value and potential. Compare to *buy-and-hold strategy*.

Mortgage. A lien on a property; commonly a loan taken out to finance the purchase of a house or property. See also *amortization*.

Multiple. A multiple is essentially the same as a *P/E ratio*. If a stock has *earnings per share* of $10 and a stock price of $200 per share, it has a P/E ratio of 20. If the stock is selling for 20 times its earnings, its multiple is said to be 20. Also called *earnings multiple*.

Municipal Bond. A bond offered by a governmental body, e.g., town or county, typically used to finance capital projects. See also *bond*.

Mutual Fund. A collection of investments, such as stocks or bonds, operated by a fund manager, of which individual investors own a portion. Mutual fund trades off the *net asset value (NAV)* that is determined at the *end* of each trading day. Compare to *exchange-traded fund*.

NASDAQ. National Association of Securities Dealers Automated Quotations. A major US *stock market*.

Neighborhood Effect. The tendency to want to match what our neighbors do or have; also known as "keeping up with the Joneses."

Net Asset Value (NAV). The price per unit of an investment at a specific time; typically used with *mutual funds* and *ETFs*.

Net Worth. Assets minus liabilities (debts); a common measure of *wealth*.

NYSE. New York Stock Exchange. A major US *stock market*.

Opportunity Cost. The foregone benefit that would have been realized from the option not chosen. Invest in stocks, or buy a boat? The one not chosen is the opportunity cost.

Options Contract. An agreement that gives the right (but not the obligation) to buy something at a specific price anytime during the life of the contract. See also *futures contract*.

P/E Ratio. See *price-to-earnings ratio*.

Passive Investing. An investing approach in which you "buy the market" (e.g., through an index fund) and let the market's overall return be your returns. Compare to *active investing*.

Personal Asset. An asset owned personally (that is, not a business asset). Common examples include checking and savings accounts, houses, personal property such as cars and household furnishings, and investments.

Personal Financial Statement (PFS). A list of your *assets* and *liabilities* that shows your *net worth*. Often used for taking out loans, such as mortgages. Similar to a business's *balance sheet*.

Portfolio Rebalancing. Periodically bringing your investment portfolio back into the intended *asset allocation* by buying or selling assets as needed.

Price-to-Earnings Ratio (P/E Ratio, P/E, PE). A company's current stock price divided by its *earnings per share* (*EPS*).

Principal. The money put into an investment or borrowed from a lender. See also *interest*.

Rate of Return. The net gain or loss on an investment over a particular period of time, often a year, expressed as a percentage. See also *real rate of return*.

Realized Gain. The profit acquired by selling an asset at a higher price than that at which it was bought. Compare to *unrealized gain*.

Real Estate. Land and structures attached to it; tends to be less liquid than investments such as stocks and bonds.

Real Estate Investment Trust (REIT). A company that manages income-producing real estate. It functions and is traded somewhat like a mutual fund, allowing investors to own real estate but maintain liquidity.

Real Rate of Return. What is earned on an investment adjusted for inflation, expressed as *rate of return* minus the *inflation rate*.

Recession. Sometimes defined as a decline in gross domestic product (GDP) for two consecutive quarters; may also be defined based on real income, production activity, and employment rates. Officially declared by the National Bureau of Economic Research. Compare to *depression*.

REIT. See *real estate investment trust*.

Registered Investment Advisor (RIA). A person or firm that advises clients on investments; they are *fiduciaries*, meaning they must act in the client's best interests.

Return on Investment (ROI). The amount made (or lost) on an investment, calculated by the gain divided by the original investment, expressed as a percentage. For example, if you invest $100 and make $9, the ROI is $9 ÷ $100 × 100 = 9%. ROI is useful in comparing investments.

Reverse Mortgage. The opposite of a mortgage: instead of paying off your loan and building home equity, you are taking money and decreasing your home equity; available only for those over 62 years of age. Compare to *mortgage*.

Revolving Credit. A form of credit that lets you repeatedly borrow up to a certain amount. Credit cards and home equity lines of credit (HELOCs) are common forms of revolving credit.

Reward. In investing, the increase in value or the return on investment (ROI). In general, low *risk*, low potential reward; higher risk, higher potential reward.

Risk. In investing, the likelihood an asset permanently loses value or shows below-expected performance. In general, low risk, low potential *reward*; higher risk, higher potential reward.

Rule of 72. The Rule of 72 tells you how long it takes to double your investment with compound interest at different rates of return. To determine how many years it will take to double your money, divide 72 by the annual interest rate. If you are making 5%, 72 ÷ 5 = 14.4 years. Prudent stock market investing should double your investment in about 10 years; that is, you want around a 7.2% return (72 ÷ 10 = 7.2).

Saver (Money Personality). Someone who tends be frugal and save a lot; they are often risk averse and keep their money in savings accounts or other "safe" investments that don't keep up with inflation. Compare to *gambler, investor, shopper,* and *spendthrift.*

Savings Account. An interest-bearing deposit account held at a bank. This is the best option for parking your emergency fund as well as holding cash for short-term needs. (However, some folks who are good savers can be overly conservative and actually have too much in a savings account.)

Security/Marketable Security. A financial instrument that can easily be turned to cash, e.g., stock, bond, and Treasury bill.

Self-Directed Investing. When you manage your own investment decisions. Compare to *advisor-managed investing.*

Self-Funding Savings. A layer of savings to develop after *emergency savings* are in place. These funds allow you to pay as you go and avoid consumer credit.

Shopper (Money Personality). Someone who tends to spend, but more carefully than the Spendthrift, as they are always in search of a "deal"; often ends up with unnecessary items because they couldn't pass up a sale. Compare to *gambler, investor, saver,* and *spendthrift.*

Simple Interest. Interest paid on principal only (not on any accumulated interest). Compare to *compound interest.*

Spendthrift (Money Personality). Someone who tends to spend money easily and even wastefully; usually has trouble saving, even with a good income. Compare to *gambler, investor, saver,* and *shopper.*

Stock. Shares represent *equity*, or ownership, in a company. Compare to *bond*.

Stock Market. The public exchanges where common stocks are bought and sold, e.g., *NYSE* and *NASDAQ*.

Strategic Purchases. Purchasing an investment in one lump sum, e.g., when you think it is a good value. Compare to *dollar-cost averaging*.

Tax Harvesting. A method of using capital losses to offset capital gains, thus reducing your tax bill. See also *capital gains tax*.

Ten-Bagger Stock. A stock that has reached ten times its original price; a baseball analogy for number of bases, e.g., a home run is a "four-bagger."

Total Return. On stocks, the combination of *appreciation* and *dividends* over a given period.

Trading. An investing approach in which traders focus on the price of the stock and its daily movement, rather than a company's fundamentals, to assess when to buy and sell. Compare to *investing*; see also *day-trading*.

Trading Platform. The online location where you have a brokerage account and do your investment transactions, e.g., Fidelity, eTrade, TD Ameritrade, Charles Schwab, Vanguard.

Treasury Securities. Investments that represent debt for the US government; also known as "Treasuries." Named in accordance with the length of time to maturity: Treasury bills ("T-bills") are up to one year; Treasury notes ("T-notes") are two to ten years; and Treasury bonds ("T-bonds") are twenty or thirty years.

Triangulation. The use of three or more objective resources to help make decisions.

Triple F (FFF). Three places not to go for investment advice: friends, family, and fools.

Under Water. Being under water means you owe more on an asset than it is worth. For example, if you have negative home equity, it means you own more on your mortgage than you could sell your house for.

Unrealized Gain. The increase in the value of an asset that has not yet been sold. Compare to *realized gain*.

Value Investing. An investing style in which you focus on purchasing undervalued stocks. Compare to *growth investing* and *income investing*.

Value Line Investment Survey. A well-known, comprehensive, subscription-based guide for individual stock investing.

Value Stock. A stock that may be undervalued; value stocks often pay regular dividends as well. Compare to *growth stock* and *income stock*.

Volatility. How much an asset's value (such as a stock price) swings up and down around its average price.

Wall Street. A real street in New York City and home of the New York Stock Exchange. Also, an umbrella term for the financial markets and the public exchanges.

Wealth. In financial terms, the primary measure of wealth is *net worth*. (In nonfinancial terms, there are, of course, many forms of wealth—family, friends, health, and so on.)

Yield. The term "yield" has multiple definitions, but most commonly it indicates what a stock investment gives you back via a dividend check. If a stock sells for $100 per share and pays a dividend of $2 per share, we say the yield is 2%. For a given year, you add the yield to the improvement in the stock price to get the *total return*.

Zero-Based Budget. A budget built from the ground up (from zero), starting with absolute necessities and carefully prioritizing non-necessities to avoid unnecessary spending.

RECOMMENDED READING

BOOKS ON PERSONAL FINANCE

The Next *Millionaire Next Door* (2018) by Sarah Stanley Fallaw, PhD, and Thomas J. Stanley, PhD. Thomas J. Stanley co-wrote the original *The Millionaire Next Door* in 1996 with William D. Danko. If your money struggle is mainly because you're guilty of "keeping up with the Joneses," this is the book for you. Key concept: Understanding how those around you, usually your neighbors or family, influence your financial behavior. (Adult peer pressure!)

The Psychology of Money (2020) by Morgan Housel. A great book about the emotions behind money-making decisions. Two takeaways: Getting money and keeping money are two different skills. Being rich is not the same as being wealthy.

Rich Dad Poor Dad (1997) by Robert T. Kiyosaki. This is a great read mainly because it will challenge your thinking. While likely no one will agree 100 percent with everything recommended, it is good to help triangulate your thinking. Best takeaway: Challenge the belief that your house is an asset. Also, all assets are not created equal.

The Richest Man in Babylon (1926) by George S. Clason. With so many life lessons included, this book is a great read for anyone; it's full of ageless wisdom. Sample takeaway: "I found the road to wealth when I decided that a part of all I earned was mine to keep."

BOOKS ON INVESTING

The Intelligent Investor (1949) by Benjamin Graham. Truly a stock market classic, it is the book that inspired Buffett and his value style of investing. It was updated in 2006 by Jason Zweig. Best key concept: Mr. Market, a sometimes-irrational personification of the market.

Margin of Safety (1991) by Seth Klarman. The intriguing thing about this book is that after selling only 5,000 copies initially, it has become a financial cult classic with copies on eBay going for $3,000 or more! I found a copy online for $200, and after reading it, I'm certain I gained well more than $200 worth of knowledge. Key concept: "Are stocks pieces of paper to be endlessly traded back and forth, or are they proportional interests in underlying businesses?"

One Up on Wall Street (1989) by Peter Lynch. Another classic by a legendary investor. His Fidelity Magellan fund was *the* fund of its time and there are still many great fundamental investing concepts throughout this book that *will* work. Key takeaways: Ten-bagger stocks and growth at a reasonable price (GARP).

The Only Investment Guide You'll Ever Need (1978) by Andrew Tobias. A classic that receives regular updated editions. One of my all-time favorites that had a real influence on me at an early age. Tobias has an entertaining style. Summary: A comprehensive guide full of money management tips.

A Random Walk Down Wall Street (1973, revised 2020) by Burton Malkiel. Another classic that states that the stock market is so efficient that it is impossible to beat the market averages on a consistent basis. I like it as an investment guide, especially Chapters 12 and 15. And the concept of keeping up with inflation is absolutely critical.

OTHER INVESTMENT RESOURCES

Brokerage account resources. Your brokerage should have some free research reports (such as Morningstar or S&P) available to you as benefit of being their customer.

Investopedia.com. Great online resource for quick answers about financial concepts. Does a terrific job of defining financial terms, with examples.

Online free reading. Kiplinger, Barron's, The Motley Fool, Yahoo Finance, and MarketWatch are all decent sites with good information, but be careful online. You must recognize when the information comes with strings attached (such as paid promotion). Stick with reputable publications and websites that have been around for a while.

The Value Line Investment Survey. This weekly newsletter, available in print or digital form, is an annual subscription of $600. This will be the best $600 dollars you'll ever spend—trust me!

The Wall Street Journal or *Investor's Business Daily.* Last but certainly not least, if you read either of these publications, you should be congratulated. They give you detailed insight into the world of business through excellent journalism.

ENDNOTES

[1] Sarah Foster, "Survey: More than half of Americans couldn't cover three months of emergency expenses with an emergency fund," Bankrate, 21 July 2021 (https://www.bankrate.com/banking/savings/emergency-savings-survey-july-2021/).

[2] "Just 26% of Americans Near or at Retirement Age Have Enough Saved for Retirement," *Schroders*, 18 March 2021 (https://www.schroders.com/en/us/media-centre/retirement-survey-2021/).

[3] Jessica Dickler, "As inflation heats up, 64% of Americans are now living paycheck to paycheck," *CNBC*, 8 March 2022 (https://www.cnbc.com/2022/03/08/as-prices-rise-64-percent-of-americans-live-paycheck-to-paycheck.html).

[4] "'The Least Wealthy 40% of Americans Have Zero Wealth': Author Michael Mechanic on Book 'Jackpot,'" *CBS News Los Angeles*, 10 May 2021 (https://www.cbsnews.com/losangeles/news/michael-mechanic-jackpot-interview/).

[5] Carmen Reinecke, "56% of American's can't cover a $1,000 emergency expense with savings," *CNBC*, 19 January 2022 (https://www.cnbc.com/2022/01/19/56percent-of-americans-cant-cover-a-1000-emergency-expense-with-savings.html).

[6] Gili Malinsky, "50% of working Americans say they live paycheck to paycheck, including 31% of those making $100,000 or more," *Grow by Acorns + CNBC*, 1 March 2022 (https://grow.acorns.com/living-paycheck-to-paycheck-how-to-break-the-cycle/).

[7] "Common sense," *American Heritage Dictionary of the English Language*, Fifth Edition (Houghton Mifflin Harcourt Publishing Company, 2016).

[8] "Common sense," English Word Information, accessed 29 June 2022 (https://wordinfo.info/unit/2806).

[9] "Personal saving rate in the United States from 1960 to 2021," Statista, 21 February 2022 (https://www.statista.com/statistics/246234/personal-savings-rate-in-the-united-states/).

[10] Christo Petrov, "20+ Incredible Personal Finance Statistics to Know in 2021," *SpendMeNot*, 6 August 2021 (https://spendmenot.com/blog/personal-finance-statistics/).

[11] "Discipline," *Lexico.com Dictionary*, accessed 31 May 2022 (https://www.lexico.com/en/definition/discipline).

[12] Sarah Berger, "Average American Spent $254 on Impulse Purchases Last 30 Days," *Magnify Money*, 28 October 2020 (https://www.magnifymoney.com/news/impulse-purchases/).

[13] Lyle Daly, "Americans' 5 Most Common Money Worries," *The Ascent by Motley Fool*, 17 July 2021 (https://www.fool.com/the-ascent/banks/articles/americans-5-most-common-money-worries/).

[14] "Big-Picture Thinking Leads to the Right Money Mindset," Capital One, 27 January 2020 (https://www.capitalone.com/about/newsroom/mind-over-money-survey/).

[15] The Organisation for Economic Co-operation and Development (OECD) is an international organization with 38 member countries that provides data, analysis, and advice on public policies and standard-setting. Member countries tend to be higher-income countries.

[16] "Household spending," OECD Data, accessed 13 March 2022 (https://data.oecd.org/hha/household-spending.htm#indicator-chart).

[17] "Household savings," OECD Data, accessed 13 March 2022 (https://data.oecd.org/hha/household-savings.htm#indicator-chart).

[18] "Household debt," OECD Data, accessed 13 March 2022 (https://data.oecd.org/hha/household-debt.htm#indicator-chart).

[19] Catey Hill, "This common behavior is the No. 1 predictor of whether you'll get divorced," *MarketWatch*, 10 January 2018 (https://www.marketwatch.com/story/this-common-behavior-is-the-no-1-predictor-of-whether-youll-get-divorced-2018-01-10).

[20] Christina Gough, "Average length of player careers in the NFL," Statista, 10 September 2019 (https:// www.statista.com/ statistics/240102/ average-player-career-length-in-the-national-football-league/).

[21] Andrew Keshner, "North Carolina is 20th state to require financial literacy class for high schoolers," *MarketWatch*, 9 July 2019 (https://www.marketwatch.com/story/more-states-consider-mandatory-financial-literacy-classes-as-high-school-students-struggle-with-basic-budgeting-2019-06-19).

[22] Olivia S. Mitchell, "A Financial Literacy Test That Works," *Forbes*, 14 December 2017 (https://www.forbes.com/sites/pensionresearchcouncil/2017/12/14/a-financial-literacy-test-that-works/).

[23] "Financial Illiteracy Cost Americans $1,389 in 2021," National Financial Educators Council, accessed 8 April 2022 (https://www.financialeducatorscouncil.org/financial-illiteracy-costs/).

[24] "United States Inflation Rate," Trading Economics, accessed 26 August 2021 (https://tradingeconomics.com/united-states/inflation-cpi).

[25] Roger Huang, "An Economic History of El Salvador's Adoption of Bitcoin," *Forbes*, 27 June 2021 (https://www.forbes.com/sites/rogerhuang/2021/06/27/an-economic-history-of-el-salvadors-adoption-of-bitcoin/?sh=61cc919093fd).

[26] "Most active stock fund managers failed to beat indexes last year," Reuters, 3 January 2022 (https://www.reuters.com/markets/asia/live-markets-most-active-stock-fund-managers-failed-beat-indexes-last-year-2022-01-03/).

ACKNOWLEDGMENTS

I would like to thank Karin Wiberg, Charles Burnett, Joe Jennings, and Steve Stephenson for their awesome support with this project. I could not have done it without them!

■■■

AUTHOR BIO

James C. Whitehurst III is President and CEO of Coastal AgroBusiness, Inc., a full-service agricultural solutions provider serving growers in the Southeast. He earned a BS in economics and business with a concentration in industrial engineering from North Carolina State University. A lifelong investor and student of personal finance, Jim is passionate about helping others build their financial literacy.

CPSIA information can be obtained
at www.ICGtesting.com
Printed in the USA
JSHW011732251122
33698JS00003B/5/J